Essential VOCA with Stories

3

Written by Michael A. Putlack • Elizabeth Lee

First Published August 2020

Publisher: Kyudo Chung
Editors: Mina Kim
Designers: Miju Yoon, Miyoung Lim
Photo Credit: www.shutterstock.com

Published and distributed by Happy House, an imprint of DARAKWON
Darakwon Bldg., 211 Moonbal-ro, Paju-si Gyeonggi-do, Korea 10881
Tel: 82-2-736-2031(Ext. 250) **Fax:** 82-2-732-2037 **Homepage:** www.ihappyhouse.co.kr

ISBN: 978-89-6653-575-0 63740
Age Range: 12 years and up
Price: ₩14,000

Components
Student Book

Free Downloadable Resources at www.ihappyhouse.co.kr
Answer Key & Translation • MP3 Files • Audio Script • Word List • Word Test

Essential VOCA with Stories

3

Table of Contents

How to Use This Book

Target Words

This section contains 20 target words. Comprehensive information about each word is provided. This includes the part of speech, one or more definitions, and one or more expressions that contain the word. There is also one or more sample sentence using the word, so readers can see how to use the word properly.

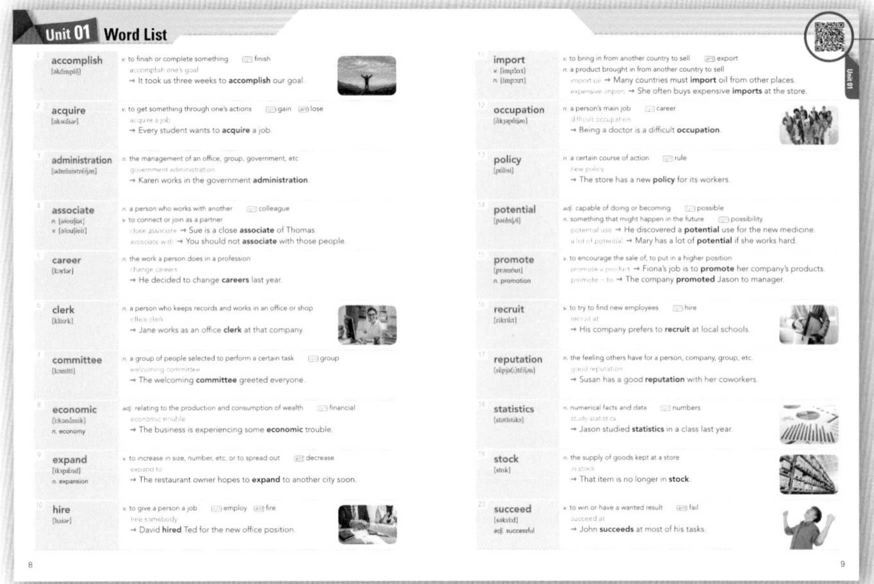

Unit 01 Word List

1 **accomplish** [əkámpliʃ]
v. to finish or complete something (syn) finish
accomplish one's goal
→ It took us three weeks to **accomplish** our goal.

2 **acquire** [əkwáiər]
v. to get something through one's actions (syn) gain (ant) lose
acquire a job
→ Every student wants to **acquire** a job.

3 **administration** [ədministréiʃən]
n. the management of an office, group, government, etc.
government administration
→ Karen works in the government **administration**.

4 **associate** n. [əsóuʃiət] v. [əsóuʃièit]
n. a person who works with another (syn) colleague
v. to connect or join as a partner
close associate → Sue is a close **associate** of Thomas.
associate with → You should not **associate** with those people.

5 **career** [kəríər]
n. the work a person does in a profession
change careers
→ He decided to change **careers** last year.

6 **clerk** [klə:rk]
n. a person who keeps records and works in an office or shop
office clerk
→ Jane works as an office **clerk** at that company.

7 **committee** [kəmíti]
n. a group of people selected to perform a certain task (syn) group
welcoming committee
→ The welcoming **committee** greeted everyone.

8 **economic** [èkənámik] n. economy
adj. relating to the production and consumption of wealth (syn) financial
economic trouble
→ The business is experiencing some **economic** trouble.

9 **expand** [ikspǽnd] n. expansion
v. to increase in size, number, etc. or to spread out (ant) decrease
expand to
→ The restaurant owner hopes to **expand** to another city soon.

10 **hire** [haiər]
v. to give a person a job (syn) employ (ant) fire
hire somebody
→ David **hired** Ted for the new office position.

8

11 **import** v. [impɔ́:rt] n. [ímpɔ:rt]
v. to bring in from another country to sell (ant) export
n. a product brought in from another country to sell
import oil → Many countries must **import** oil from other places.
expensive import → She often buys expensive **imports** at the store.

12 **occupation** [àkjəpéiʃən]
n. a person's main job (syn) career
difficult occupation
→ Being a doctor is a difficult **occupation**.

13 **policy** [páləsi]
n. a certain course of action (syn) rule
new policy
→ The store has a new **policy** for its workers.

14 **potential** [pəténʃəl]
adj. capable of doing or becoming (syn) possible
n. something that might happen in the future (syn) possibility
potential use → He discovered a **potential** use for the new medicine.
a lot of potential → Mary has a lot of **potential** if she works hard.

15 **promote** [prəmóut] n. promotion
v. to encourage the sale of; to put in a higher position
promote a product → Fiona's job is to **promote** her company's products.
promote ~ to → The company **promoted** Jason to manager.

16 **recruit** [rikrú:t]
v. to try to find new employees (syn) hire
recruit at
→ His company prefers to **recruit** at local schools.

17 **reputation** [rèpjə(:)téiʃən]
n. the feeling others have for a person, company, group, etc.
good reputation
→ Susan has a good **reputation** with her coworkers.

18 **statistics** [stətístiks]
n. numerical facts and data (syn) numbers
study statistics
→ Jason studied **statistics** in a class last year.

19 **stock** [stak]
n. the supply of goods kept at a store
in stock
→ That item is no longer in **stock**.

20 **succeed** [səksí:d] adj. successful
v. to win or have a wanted result (ant) fail
succeed at
→ John **succeeds** at most of his tasks.

Unit 01

9

QR cord

Readers can use the QR code to listen to audio recordings of the words and examples sentences.

Unit Exercises

There are a wide variety of exercises for readers to practice the words they learn in Word List. The exercises give readers the opportunity to test their knowledge of the definitions of the words and how the words are used in sentences. There is also a short reading passage containing target words from the unit. Following it are 4 comprehension questions to make sure that readers understand the passage.

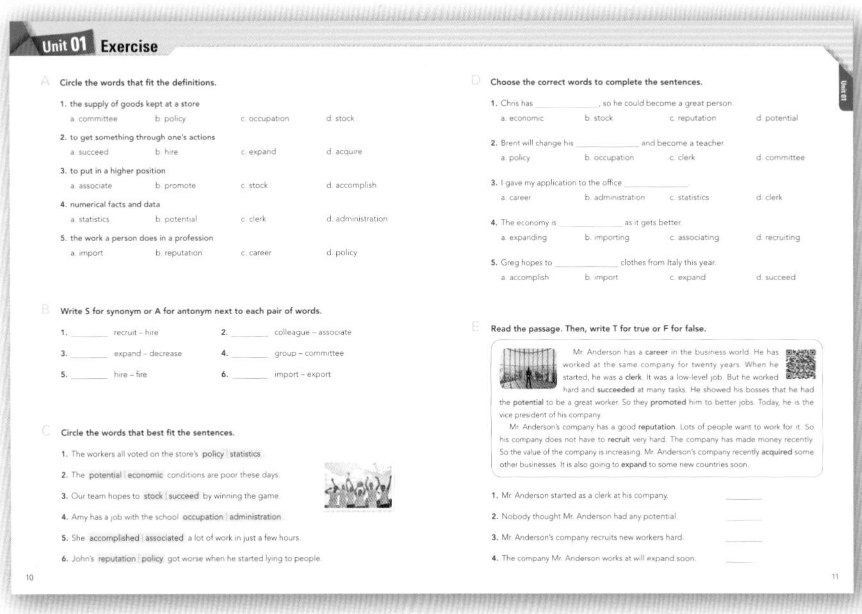

Unit 01 Exercise

A Circle the words that fit the definitions.

1. the supply of goods kept at a store
   a. committee b. policy c. occupation d. stock
2. to get something through one's actions
   a. succeed b. hire c. expand d. acquire
3. to put in a higher position
   a. associate b. promote c. stock d. accomplish
4. numerical facts and data
   a. statistics b. potential c. clerk d. administration
5. the work a person does in a profession
   a. import b. reputation c. career d. policy

B Write S for synonym or A for antonym next to each pair of words.

1. ______ recruit – hire
2. ______ colleague – associate
3. ______ expand – decrease
4. ______ group – committee
5. ______ hire – fire
6. ______ import – export

C Circle the words that best fit the sentences.

1. The workers all voted on the store's policy | statistics.
2. The potential | economic conditions are poor these days.
3. Our team hopes to stock | succeed by winning the game.
4. Amy has a job with the school occupation | administration.
5. She accomplished | associated a lot of work in just a few hours.
6. John's reputation | policy got worse when he started lying to people.

10

D Choose the correct words to complete the sentences.

1. Chris has ______, so he could become a great person.
   a. economic b. stock c. reputation d. potential
2. Brent will change his ______ and become a teacher.
   a. policy b. occupation c. clerk d. committee
3. I gave my application to the office ______.
   a. career b. administration c. statistics d. clerk
4. The economy is ______ as it gets better.
   a. expanding b. importing c. associating d. recruiting
5. Greg hopes to ______ clothes from Italy this year.
   a. accomplish b. import c. expand d. succeed

E Read the passage. Then, write T for true or F for false.

Mr. Anderson has a **career** in the business world. He has worked at the same company for twenty years. When he started, he was a **clerk**. It was a low-level job. But he worked hard and **succeeded** at many tasks. He showed his bosses that he had the **potential** to be a great worker. So they **promoted** him to better jobs. Today, he is the vice president of his company.

Mr. Anderson's company has a good **reputation**. Lots of people want to work for it. So his company does not have to **recruit** very hard. The company has made money recently. So the value of the company is increasing. Mr. Anderson's company recently **acquired** some other businesses. It is also going to **expand** to some new countries soon.

1. Mr. Anderson started as a clerk at his company. ______
2. Nobody thought Mr. Anderson had any potential. ______
3. Mr. Anderson's company recruits new workers hard. ______
4. The company Mr. Anderson works at will expand soon. ______

Unit 01

11

Review Units

After every five units, there is a review unit. This section retests readers on the knowledge they learned in the previous units. There are exercises that test readers on definitions and word usage. Each review unit also contains a crossword puzzle and a reading passage containing target words. Readers must then answer comprehension questions testing their understanding of the passage.

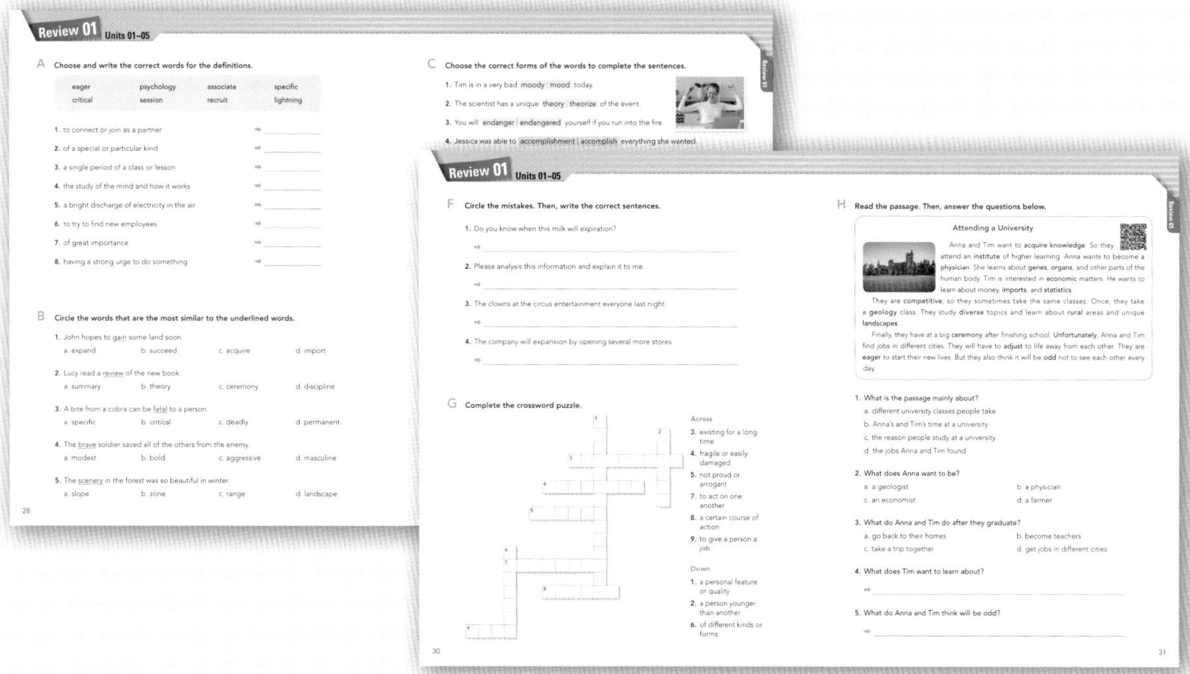

Index

The index contains all of the words in each unit. Readers can use it to search for words while studying.

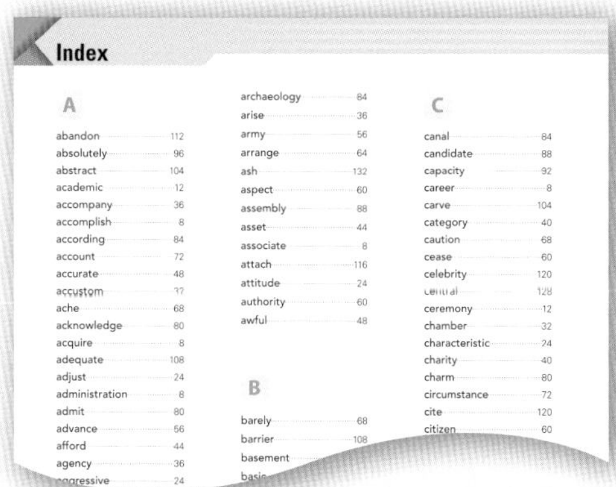

Answer Key & Translation

The answer key and Korean translation may be downloaded for free at www.ihappyhouse.co.kr.

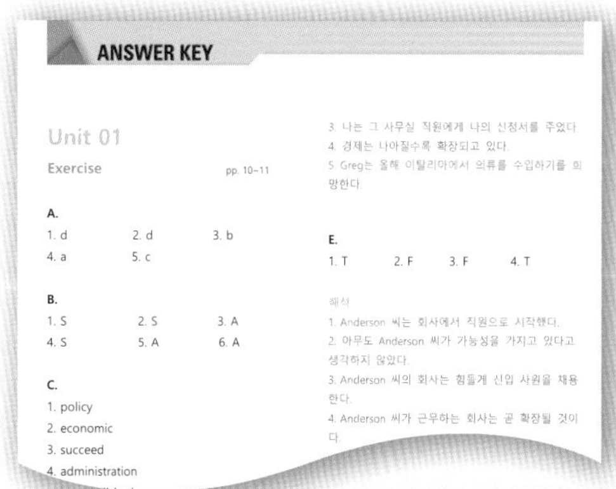

Part of Speech Abbreviations	•noun = *n.* •verb = *v.* •adjective = *adj.* •adverb = *adv.* •preposition = *prep.* •pronoun = *pron.* •conjunction = *con.* •plural = *pl.*

Unit 01 Word List

1 **accomplish** [əkámpliʃ]
v. to finish or complete something (syn) finish
accomplish one's goal
→ It took us three weeks to **accomplish** our goal.

2 **acquire** [əkwáiər]
v. to get something through one's actions (syn) gain (ant) lose
acquire a job
→ Every student wants to **acquire** a job.

3 **administration** [ədmìnistréiʃən]
n. the management of an office, group, government, etc.
government administration
→ Karen works in the government **administration**.

4 **associate** *n.* [əśouʃiət] *v.* [əśouʃieit]
n. a person who works with another (syn) colleague
v. to connect or join as a partner
close associate → Sue is a close **associate** of Thomas.
associate with → You should not **associate** with those people.

5 **career** [kəríər]
n. the work a person does in a profession
change careers
→ He decided to change **careers** last year.

6 **clerk** [kləːrk]
n. a person who keeps records and works in an office or shop
office clerk
→ Jane works as an office **clerk** at that company.

7 **committee** [kəmíti]
n. a group of people selected to perform a certain task (syn) group
welcoming committee
→ The welcoming **committee** greeted everyone.

8 **economic** [ìːkənámik] *n.* economy
adj. relating to the production and consumption of wealth (syn) financial
economic trouble
→ The business is experiencing some **economic** trouble.

9 **expand** [ikspǽnd] *n.* expansion
v. to increase in size, number, etc. or to spread out (ant) decrease
expand to
→ The restaurant owner hopes to **expand** to another city soon.

10 **hire** [haiər]
v. to give a person a job (syn) employ (ant) fire
hire somebody
→ David **hired** Ted for the new office position.

11 **import**
v. [impɔ́ːrt]
n. [ímpɔːrt]

v. to bring in from another country to sell (ant) export
n. a product brought in from another country to sell
import oil → Many countries must **import** oil from other places.
expensive import → She often buys expensive **imports** at the store.

12 **occupation**
[àkjəpéiʃən]

n. a person's main job (syn) career
difficult occupation
→ Being a doctor is a difficult **occupation**.

13 **policy**
[pálisi]

n. a certain course of action (syn) rule
new policy
→ The store has a new **policy** for its workers.

14 **potential**
[pəténʃəl]

adj. capable of doing or becoming (syn) possible
n. something that might happen in the future (syn) possibility
potential use → He discovered a **potential** use for the new medicine.
a lot of potential → Mary has a lot of **potential** if she works hard.

15 **promote**
[prəmóut]
n. promotion

v. to encourage the sale of; to put in a higher position
promote a product → Fiona's job is to **promote** her company's products.
promote ~ to → The company **promoted** Jason to manager.

16 **recruit**
[rikrúːt]

v. to try to find new employees (syn) hire
recruit at
→ His company prefers to **recruit** at local schools.

17 **reputation**
[rèpjə(ː)téiʃən]

n. the feeling others have for a person, company, group, etc.
good reputation
→ Susan has a good **reputation** with her coworkers.

18 **statistics**
[stətístiks]

n. numerical facts and data (syn) numbers
study statistics
→ Jason studied **statistics** in a class last year.

19 **stock**
[stak]

n. the supply of goods kept at a store
in stock
→ That item is no longer in **stock**.

20 **succeed**
[səksíːd]
adj. successful

v. to win or have a wanted result (ant) fail
succeed at
→ John **succeeds** at most of his tasks.

Unit 01 Exercise

A Circle the words that fit the definitions.

1. the supply of goods kept at a store

a. committee b. policy c. occupation d. stock

2. to get something through one's actions

a. succeed b. hire c. expand d. acquire

3. to put in a higher position

a. associate b. promote c. stock d. accomplish

4. numerical facts and data

a. statistics b. potential c. clerk d. administration

5. the work a person does in a profession

a. import b. reputation c. career d. policy

B Write S for synonym or A for antonym next to each pair of words.

1. ________ recruit – hire

2. ________ colleague – associate

3. ________ expand – decrease

4. ________ group – committee

5. ________ hire – fire

6. ________ import – export

C Circle the words that best fit the sentences.

1. The workers all voted on the store's policy | statistics .

2. The potential | economic conditions are poor these days.

3. Our team hopes to stock | succeed by winning the game.

4. Amy has a job with the school occupation | administration .

5. She accomplished | associated a lot of work in just a few hours.

6. John's reputation | policy got worse when he started lying to people.

D Choose the correct words to complete the sentences.

1. Chris has ______________, so he could become a great person.

a. economic b. stock c. reputation d. potential

2. Brent will change his ______________ and become a teacher.

a. policy b. occupation c. clerk d. committee

3. I gave my application to the office ______________.

a. career b. administration c. statistics d. clerk

4. The economy is ______________ as it gets better.

a. expanding b. importing c. associating d. recruiting

5. Greg hopes to ______________ clothes from Italy this year.

a. accomplish b. import c. expand d. succeed

E Read the passage. Then, write T for true or F for false.

Mr. Anderson has a **career** in the business world. He has worked at the same company for twenty years. When he started, he was a **clerk**. It was a low-level job. But he worked hard and **succeeded** at many tasks. He showed his bosses that he had the **potential** to be a great worker. So they **promoted** him to better jobs. Today, he is the vice president of his company.

Mr. Anderson's company has a good **reputation**. Lots of people want to work for it. So his company does not have to **recruit** very hard. The company has made money recently. So the value of the company is increasing. Mr. Anderson's company recently **acquired** some other businesses. It is also going to **expand** to some new countries soon.

1. Mr. Anderson started as a clerk at his company. ________

2. Nobody thought Mr. Anderson had any potential. ________

3. Mr. Anderson's company recruits new workers hard. ________

4. The company Mr. Anderson works at will expand soon. ________

Unit 02 Word List

1 **academic**
[ækədémik]
n. academy

adj. relating to a college, school, etc.
academic performance
→ Suzy's **academic** performance this year was excellent.

2 **analyze**
[ǽnəlàiz]
n. analysis

v. to look at carefully and in detail
analyze data
→ We can solve the problem by **analyzing** the data.

3 **basic**
[béisik]

adj. simple (ant) complicated
basic math
→ Students learn **basic** math in first grade.

4 **ceremony**
[sérəmòuni]

n. a formal activity held for a special occasion
graduation ceremony
→ The school's graduation **ceremony** is this Friday.

5 **confuse**
[kənfjú:z]
n. confusion

v. to make unclear or to puzzle someone (ant) explain
confuse someone
→ The teacher's explanation **confused** the students.

6 **competitive**
[kəmpétitiv]
n. competition

adj. having a strong urge to succeed or win (ant) uncompetitive
competitive game
→ It is a **competitive** game as both teams are good.

7 **discipline**
[dísəplin]

n. punishment used to correct behavior; training to follow certain rules
physical discipline → Most schools do not use physical **discipline** now.
learn a discipline → He is learning a **discipline** connected to computers.

8 **enthusiasm**
[inθjú:ziæ̀zəm]
adj. enthusiastic

n. the act of being very interested in an activity (syn) passion
great enthusiasm
→ Kay has great **enthusiasm** for playing the flute.

9 **essay**
[ései]

n. a short piece of writing on a certain topic or theme
write an essay
→ Dave wrote an **essay** on his future goals.

10 **interact**
[intərǽkt]

v. to act on one another (syn) connect
interact with
→ The students **interact** with children from other countries.

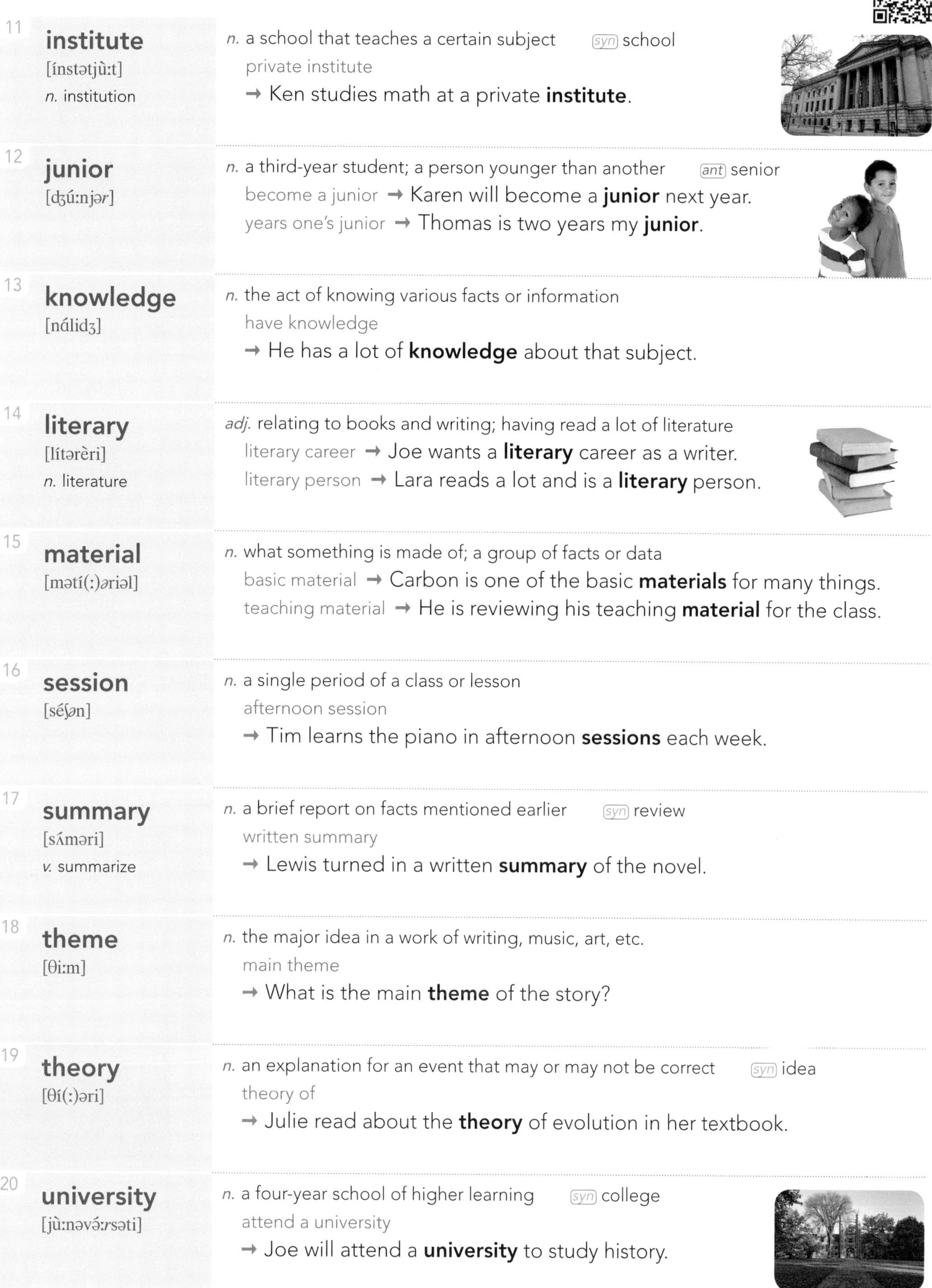

11 **institute**
[ínstətjù:t]
n. institution

n. a school that teaches a certain subject (syn) school
private institute
→ Ken studies math at a private **institute**.

12 **junior**
[dʒú:njər]

n. a third-year student; a person younger than another (ant) senior
become a junior → Karen will become a **junior** next year.
years one's junior → Thomas is two years my **junior**.

13 **knowledge**
[nálidʒ]

n. the act of knowing various facts or information
have knowledge
→ He has a lot of **knowledge** about that subject.

14 **literary**
[lítərèri]
n. literature

adj. relating to books and writing; having read a lot of literature
literary career → Joe wants a **literary** career as a writer.
literary person → Lara reads a lot and is a **literary** person.

15 **material**
[mətí(:)əriəl]

n. what something is made of; a group of facts or data
basic material → Carbon is one of the basic **materials** for many things.
teaching material → He is reviewing his teaching **material** for the class.

16 **session**
[séʃən]

n. a single period of a class or lesson
afternoon session
→ Tim learns the piano in afternoon **sessions** each week.

17 **summary**
[sʌ́məri]
v. summarize

n. a brief report on facts mentioned earlier (syn) review
written summary
→ Lewis turned in a written **summary** of the novel.

18 **theme**
[θi:m]

n. the major idea in a work of writing, music, art, etc.
main theme
→ What is the main **theme** of the story?

19 **theory**
[θí(:)əri]

n. an explanation for an event that may or may not be correct (syn) idea
theory of
→ Julie read about the **theory** of evolution in her textbook.

20 **university**
[jù:nəvə́:rsəti]

n. a four-year school of higher learning (syn) college
attend a university
→ Joe will attend a **university** to study history.

Unit 02 Exercise

A Match the words with their definitions.

1. essay	a. a single period of a class or lesson
2. theme	b. the major idea in a work of writing, music, art, etc.
3. ceremony	c. a four-year school of higher learning
4. analyze	d. to act on one another
5. session	e. a short piece of writing on a certain topic or theme
6. interact	f. the act of knowing various facts or information
7. knowledge	g. a formal activity held for a special occasion
8. university	h. to look at carefully and in detail

B Circle the two words in each group that are opposites.

1.	a. competitive	b. literary	c. uncompetitive	d. institute
2.	a. essay	b. senior	c. junior	d. summary
3.	a. knowledge	b. material	c. confuse	d. explain
4.	a. complicated	b. ceremony	c. basic	d. theme

C Circle the words that best fit the sentences.

1. His academic | basic studies at the school were very good.
2. The teacher gave the students some study material | theory .
3. Greg came up with a new theory | session in science.
4. You must read the book and write a summary | material of it.
5. Eric opened a math ceremony | institute for young students.
6. Jane's discipline | enthusiasm for the play made everyone excited.

Unit 02

D Choose the correct words to complete the sentences.

1. Teachers expect good ______________ from their students.
   a. theory b. discipline c. ceremony d. university

2. He wrote a ______________ work on the plays of Shakespeare.
   a. knowledge b. enthusiasm c. theme d. literary

3. Most of the players on the team are ______________.
   a. competitive b. basic c. summary d. academic

4. You can solve this problem in three ______________ steps.
   a. basic b. session c. competitive d. theory

5. All of the ______________ are looking forward to their senior year.
   a. institutes b. junior c. universities d. summaries

E Read the passage. Then, fill in the blanks.

There are many places for students to study after high school. Lots of students study at **universities** for four years and then graduate. At **universities**, students **interact** with others. Some learn **basic** concepts. Others study **academic** topics. The students write **essays**, learn various **theories**, and take tests. Lots of **university** students are very **competitive**.

Other students attend private **institutes**. At these places, they can acquire all kinds of **knowledge**. Some study languages while others learn math, science, history, or other subjects. Students at **institutes** attend sessions a few days a week. Most of them have a lot of **enthusiasm** for learning. The **material** they learn can help them get jobs. Thanks to **universities** and **institutes**, students around the world can improve their **knowledge** of many subjects.

1. Students can ______________ with other students at universities.

2. Students at universities take tests and learn various ______________.

3. At private institutes, students attend ______________ a few days a week.

4. Students can get ______________ at both universities and institutes.

Unit 03 Word List

1 **agriculture** [ǽgrəkʌ̀ltʃər]

n. the act of growing crops and raising animals (syn) farming

work in agriculture

→ Many people in this area work in **agriculture**.

2 **cliff** [klif]

n. a high side of a mountain or hill that goes almost straight up

dangerous cliff

→ Yosemite has many dangerous **cliffs**.

3 **crop** [krɑp]

n. a plant that a farmer grows

harvest one's crop

→ Many farmers harvest their **crops** in fall.

4 **decay** [dikéi]

v. to break down and to fall apart (syn) rot

decay slowly

→ Most plants **decay** slowly over time.

5 **decrease** [díːkriːs]

v. to become less in size, amount, etc. (ant) increase

decrease in

→ Pollution in the area is **decreasing** in amount.

6 **diverse** [divə́ːrs], [dáivərs]

n. diversity

adj. of different kinds or forms (syn) various

diverse plants

→ **Diverse** plants grow in the world's rainforests.

7 **endanger** [indéindʒər]

adj. endangered

v. to make someone or something be at risk

endanger the environment

→ We are **endangering** the environment with pollution.

8 **evaporate** [ivǽpərèit]

v. to change from a liquid to a gas (syn) disappear

evaporate quickly

→ Water **evaporates** quickly at 100 degrees Celsius.

9 **ferment** [fə́ːrment]

v. to change in form from sugar to alcohol

ferment grapes

→ People **ferment** grapes to create wine.

10 **fuel** [fjú(ː)əl]

n. matter such as wood, coal, or gas that burns to create heat or power

jet fuel

→ Planes need jet **fuel** to fly in the air.

11 **geology** [dʒiάlədʒi]

n. the study of the Earth and the rocks and the soil on it

study geology

→ Larry hopes to study **geology** at his university.

12 **iron** [áiərn]

n. a hard element used to make tools and steel

melt iron

→ You must use a lot of heat to melt **iron**.

13 **landscape** [lǽndskèip]

n. an area of land that a person can see from one point (syn) scenery

beautiful landscape

→ They saw beautiful **landscapes** in the countryside.

14 **lightning** [láitniŋ]

n. a bright discharge of electricity in the air

thunder and lightning

→ The storm brought thunder and **lightning** all night long.

15 **mild** [maild]

adj. not strong or extreme (syn) calm

mild weather

→ This region gets **mild** weather in spring and fall.

16 **range** [reindʒ]

n. the degree of the action of something; an area of wide, open land

wide range of → Irene's interests cover a wide **range** of subjects.

on the range → Many cows are grazing on the **range**.

17 **rural** [rú(:)ərəl]

adj. relating to the countryside (ant) urban

rural life

→ **Rural** life is more relaxing than life in the city.

18 **scarce** [skεərs]

n. scarcity

adj. not common or enough (syn) rare (ant) plentiful

be scarce

→ Water is **scarce** during a drought.

19 **slope** [sloup]

n. ground that has a sharp angle

steep slope

→ It was difficult to walk up the steep **slope**.

20 **zone** [zoun]

n. an area different in some way from the land around it (syn) region

dangerous zone

→ Because of the flood, they were in a dangerous **zone**.

Unit 03 Exercise

A Circle the words that fit the definitions.

1. ground that has a sharp angle

a. agriculture b. slope c. fuel d. zone

2. a plant that a farmer grows

a. crop b. agriculture c. cliff d. geology

3. a bright discharge of electricity in the air

a. iron b. landscape c. slope d. lightning

4. to make someone or something be at risk

a. ferment b. decrease c. evaporate d. endanger

5. not strong or extreme

a. diverse b. mild c. scarce d. rural

B Choose and write the correct words for the blanks.

decrease	diverse	decay	landscape	rural	scarce

1. scenery = ____________ **2.** increase ≠ ____________

3. plentiful ≠ ____________ **4.** rot = ____________

5. various = ____________ **6.** urban ≠ ____________

C Circle the words that best fit the sentences.

1. It can be difficult to climb up a crop | cliff .

2. She lives in a hot tropical cliff | zone with her family.

3. I stopped at the gas station to put iron | fuel into my car.

4. It is so hot that water is evaporating | decaying very quickly.

5. The airplane has a range | landscape of thousands of kilometers.

6. People evaporate | ferment vegetables in order to make kimchi.

D Choose the correct words to complete the sentences.

1. Chet hopes to study ______________ at his university.
   a. range b. slope c. zone d. geology

2. The farmer has a big interest in ______________.
   a. agriculture b. cliff c. iron d. range

3. A person must use ______________ in order to make steel.
   a. iron b. geology c. lightning d. crop

4. Food was ______________ during the long winter months.
   a. rural b. mild c. scarce d. diverse

5. He loved looking at the ______________ as the train went through the area.
   a. fuel b. crop c. landscape d. agriculture

E Read the passage. Then, write T for true or F for false.

Land in **rural** areas is different from land in cities. In **rural** areas, there is a lot of **agriculture**. Farmers grow all kinds of **crops** in their fields. They grow these **crops** to sell to people in other places. Some farmers plant just one kind of **crop**, such as rice or wheat. Other farmers plant a **diverse** number of crops, such as corn, potatoes, carrots, and peas.

The **geology** in **rural** areas is unique, too. There are some mountains in **rural** areas. They often have **cliffs**. Other **rural** areas have hills with gentle **slopes**. The **landscape** in these **zones** is often beautiful. The weather can be **mild** as well. Sadly, some **rural** areas are **endangered**. They are **decreasing** in number since people are not protecting the environment.

1. Farmers in rural areas always grow just one kind of crop. ________
2. There are some mountains in rural areas. ________
3. There is not any mild weather in rural areas. ________
4. Rural areas are endangered because of some people. ________

Unit 04 Word List

1 **anxiety**
[æŋzáiəti]
adj. anxious

n. uneasiness of the mind caused by danger or fear (syn) worry
experience anxiety
→ Jake experienced **anxiety** because of his exams.

2 **beneficial**
[bènəfíʃəl]

n. providing an advantage or something positive (ant) harmful
beneficial to
→ Vitamins are **beneficial** to people's health.

3 **consult**
[kánsʌlt]

v. to ask someone for help, guidance, or advice
consult with
→ The patient will **consult** with the doctor to find out the problem.

4 **critical**
[krítikəl]

adj. of great importance; serious
critical condition → The sick man is in **critical** condition.
critical moment → This is a **critical** moment in Rita's life.

5 **deadly**
[dédli]

adj. causing death (syn) fatal
deadly poison
→ You should not drink that **deadly** poison.

6 **delicate**
[délәkit]

adj. fragile or easily damaged (ant) tough
delicate creature
→ It is a **delicate** creature that can die easily.

7 **drown**
[draun]
drown - drowned - drowned

v. to die from being under water
drown in
→ The young boys **drowned** in the ocean.

8 **evaluate**
[ivǽljuèit]
n. evaluation

v. to determine the value or condition of (syn) assess
evaluate the results
→ She must **evaluate** the results of the test.

9 **expire**
[ikspáiər]
n. expiration

v. to run out of time; to come to an end or die
expire soon
→ This food is going to **expire** soon.

10 **gene**
[dʒi:n]

n. the basic unit of heredity
gene therapy
→ **Gene** therapy is a new field in science these days.

11 **monitor**
[mɑ́nətər]
monitor - monitored - monitored

v. to watch over carefully
n. the screen of a computer
monitor someone → The doctors are carefully **monitoring** the patient.
computer monitor → There is a problem with my computer **monitor**.

12 **mood**
[mu:d]

n. a state or feeling at a certain time
good mood
→ Terry is in a good **mood** today.

13 **mortal**
[mɔ́:rtəl]
n. mortality

adj. able to die
mortal life
→ All creatures have a **mortal** life.

14 **organ**
[ɔ́:rgən]

n. a group of tissues in the body that have a certain task
vital organ
→ The heart and the lungs are both vital **organs**.

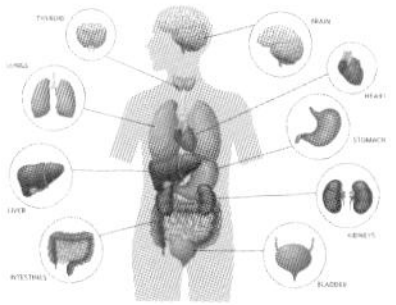

15 **permanent**
[pə́:rmənənt]

adj. existing for a long time (syn) lasting (ant) brief
permanent ink
→ This pen uses **permanent** ink.

16 **physician**
[fizíʃən]

n. a person who is qualified to practice medicine (syn) doctor
personal physician
→ She visits her personal **physician** when she is sick.

17 **specific**
[spisífik]

adj. of a special or particular kind
specific reason
→ What is the **specific** reason you want to move?

18 **symptom**
[símptəm]

n. a problem caused by a certain disease (syn) sign
minor symptom
→ He has some minor **symptoms** from his illness.

Symptoms of CORONAVIRUS (COVID-19)
Fever
Shortness of breath
Cough

19 **unfortunately**
[ʌnfɔ́:rtʃənitli]

adv. unluckily (ant) fortunately
quite unfortunately
→ Quite **unfortunately**, Sue became very sick.

20 **victim**
[víktim]

n. a person who is hurt or killed in an accident
victim of
→ He was a **victim** of a fire.

Unit 04 Exercise

A Match the words with their definitions.

1. expire • • a. the basic unit of heredity
2. mood • • b. of a special or particular kind
3. gene • • c. a state or feeling at a certain time
4. physician • • d. the screen of a computer
5. mortal • • e. of great importance
6. critical • • f. a person who is qualified to practice medicine
7. specific • • g. able to die
8. monitor • • h. to run out of time

B Circle the two words in each group that have the same meaning.

1. a. sign	b. organ	c. physician	d. symptom
2. a. mortal	b. permanent	c. lasting	d. critical
3. a. worry	b. anxiety	c. specific	d. unfortunately
4. a. expire	b. evaluate	c. drown	d. assess

C Circle the words that best fit the sentences.

1. There were three genes | victims in the car crash.
2. Exercising more would be beneficial | mortal to you.
3. The artwork is specific | delicate and can easily break.
4. I need to monitor | consult with an expert right now.
5. She almost drowned | evaluated while swimming in the ocean.
6. The disease affects some of the symptoms | organs in the body.

D Choose the correct words to complete the sentences.

1. He did not give a ______________ time for his arrival.
   a. permanent　　b. specific　　c. critical　　d. mortal

2. ______________, nobody answered the question correctly.
   a. Gene　　b. Beneficial　　c. Physician　　d. Unfortunately

3. She experiences ______________ and cannot speak in public.
   a. organ　　b. mood　　c. anxiety　　d. gene

4. The illness caused ______________ damage to his body.
   a. delicate　　b. unfortunately　　c. beneficial　　d. permanent

5. The doctor will ______________ the patient soon.
   a. expire　　b. evaluate　　c. drown　　d. symptom

E Read the passage. Then, fill in the blanks.

Good health is important. All humans are **mortal**, so they will eventually die. But while they are alive, they can have healthy lives. It is **critical** that people see a **physician** regularly. The doctor can give them a checkup. That way, the **physician** can **evaluate** the physical condition of each person. If there is a problem, the doctor can **monitor** it until it gets better. This is **beneficial** to people.

Unfortunately, most people do not regularly **consult** with a **physician**. So they may develop big problems. When their **symptoms** become bad, they finally visit a doctor. Some people have **anxiety** when they are sick. They believe they have a **deadly** disease and will **expire** soon. These people can be in bad **moods** at the doctor's office.

1. People should see a ______________ regularly for a checkup.
2. A doctor can ______________ people until they get better.
3. Most people do not ______________ with a doctor regularly.
4. People can be in bad ______________ when they are visiting the doctor.

Unit 05 Word List

1 **adjust**
[ədʒʌ́st]
n. adjustment

v. to change something to improve it
adjust to
→ Ted needs to **adjust** to life in another country.

2 **aggressive**
[əgrésiv]

adj. tending to make sudden attacks; trying hard to win
be aggressive → The country is **aggressive** toward its enemies.
aggressive player → Jane is an **aggressive** volleyball player.

3 **amuse**
[əmjú:z]
amuse - amused - amused

v. to make someone laugh
amuse a crowd
→ The comedian knows how to **amuse** a crowd.

4 **attitude**
[ǽtitjù:d]

n. a feeling or position toward someone or something
positive attitude
→ Russ has a positive **attitude** in science class.

5 **bold**
[bould]

adj. not afraid in dangerous situations (syn) brave
bold man
→ The **bold** man saved the baby from the fire.

6 **characteristic**
[kæ̀riktərístik]

n. a personal feature or quality (syn) personality
main characteristic
→ Please describe your main **characteristic**.

7 **complex**
[kámpleks]

adj. composed of many parts (ant) simple
complex personality
→ Susan has a very **complex** personality.

8 **dislike**
[disláik]

v. to feel displeasure toward (syn) hate (ant) like
dislike someone
→ Larry really **dislikes** Sam.

9 **eager**
[í:gər]

adj. having a strong urge to do something
eager to
→ We are **eager** to see the new movie.

10 **entertain**
[èntərtéin]
n. entertainment

v. to amuse other people (syn) amuse (ant) bore
entertain an audience
→ The TV program really **entertained** the audience.

11 **humble** [hʌmbl]

adj. not proud or arrogant (syn) modest

humble person

→ Ellen is such a **humble** person.

12 **masculine** [mǽskjəlin]

adj. having the qualities or characteristics of a man (ant) feminine

masculine role

→ Some cultures have **masculine** roles for men in marriage.

13 **modest** [mádist]

adj. having a humble view of one's worth (ant) proud

modest behavior

→ Your modest **behavior** is attractive to people.

14 **odd** [ɑd]

adj. different from what is normal or expected (syn) strange

odd comment

→ She sometimes makes **odd** comments to her friends.

15 **patience** [péiʃəns]

n. the ability to wait without getting upset

a lot of patience

→ Fishing requires a lot of **patience**.

16 **psychology** [saikálədʒi]

n. the study of the mind and how it works

major in psychology

→ Ken hopes to major in **psychology** at college.

17 **romantic** [roumǽntik]

adj. relating to feelings of love

romantic movie

→ Deanna enjoys watching **romantic** movies.

18 **stereotype** [stériətàip]
adj. stereotypical

n. a simplified image of a group that is held by many people

believe in a stereotype

→ Many people believe in **stereotypes** about other cultures.

19 **temper** [témpər]

n. a certain state of mind or feelings (syn) mood

bad temper

→ Rachel has a bad **temper** and gets mad easily.

20 **vain** [vein]

adj. without value

in vain

→ His attempt to win the game was in **vain**.

Unit 05 Exercise

A Circle the correct definitions for the given words.

1. aggressive

a. not proud or arrogant
b. trying hard to win
c. relating to feelings of love
d. composed of many parts

2. psychology

a. a personal feature or quality
b. the ability to wait without getting upset
c. the study of the mind and how it works
d. a feeling or position toward someone or something

3. odd

a. different from what is normal or expected
b. tending to make sudden attacks
c. having the qualities or characteristics of a man
d. not afraid in dangerous situations

4. vain

a. without value
b. having a humble view of one's worth
c. composed of many parts or complicated
d. having a strong urge to do something

B Write S for synonym or A for antonym next to each pair of words.

1. ________ simple – complex
2. ________ modest – proud
3. ________ temper – mood
4. ________ feminine – masculine
5. ________ bold – brave
6. ________ amuse – entertain

C Circle the words that best fit the sentences.

1. I entertain | dislike having to take the bus.

2. You should be romantic | humble and not brag.

3. Please amuse | adjust the position of the machine.

4. Glenn has a bad attitude | characteristic toward his job.

5. You need patience | mood to be able to sit and wait for hours.

6. There are many stereotypes | patience about people from other countries.

D Choose the correct words to complete the sentences.

1. Everyone is _______________ to finish the project.

a. eager b. complex c. vain d. humble

2. She is _______________ and loves to get flowers as presents.

a. masculine b. romantic c. aggressive d. odd

3. I _______________ my friends by telling them some jokes.

a. amused b. adjusted c. tempered d. disliked

4. His best _______________ is his loyalty to his friends.

a. patience b. temper c. stereotype d. characteristic

5. Chris was _______________ for trying to stop the men from fighting.

a. modest b. bold c. romantic d. eager

E Read the passage. Then, write T for true or F for false.

People have various **characteristics**. These make people different from others. For example, some **masculine** men can be **bold** and **aggressive**. In some cases, they have bad **tempers**, so they get angry easily. Some people like this kind of personality, but others **dislike** it. On the other hand, many men may be **modest** and **humble**. Instead of being **aggressive**, they have a lot of **patience**. These men are often **eager** to please others and enjoy **entertaining** their friends.

It can be difficult for some people to **adjust** to others with different personalities. They find it **odd** that people can be so different. Some decide to study **psychology** to learn about how humans act. It teaches them about the different **attitudes** people have. They learn how **complex** most humans are as well.

1. Some masculine men are bold and have bad tempers. _______

2. Some men are humble while others are aggressive. _______

3. People can easily adjust to others with different personalities. _______

4. People who study psychology do not learn about how humans act. _______

Review 01 Units 01~05

A Choose and write the correct words for the definitions.

eager	psychology	associate	specific
critical	session	recruit	lightning

1. to connect or join as a partner ➡ ______________
2. of a special or particular kind ➡ ______________
3. a single period of a class or lesson ➡ ______________
4. the study of the mind and how it works ➡ ______________
5. a bright discharge of electricity in the air ➡ ______________
6. to try to find new employees ➡ ______________
7. of great importance ➡ ______________
8. having a strong urge to do something ➡ ______________

B Circle the words that are the most similar to the underlined words.

1. John hopes to <u>gain</u> some land soon.
   a. expand b. succeed c. acquire d. import

2. Lucy read a <u>review</u> of the new book.
   a. summary b. theory c. ceremony d. discipline

3. A bite from a cobra can be <u>fatal</u> to a person.
   a. specific b. critical c. deadly d. permanent

4. The <u>brave</u> soldier saved all of the others from the enemy.
   a. modest b. bold c. aggressive d. masculine

5. The <u>scenery</u> in the forest was so beautiful in winter.
   a. slope b. zone c. range d. landscape

C Choose the correct forms of the words to complete the sentences.

1. Tim is in a very bad moody | mood today.
2. The scientist has a unique theory | theorize of the event.
3. You will endanger | endangered yourself if you run into the fire.
4. Jessica was able to accomplishment | accomplish everything she wanted.
5. That man believes many stereotypes | stereotypical about different people.

D Complete the sentences with the words in the box.

attitude
fuel
unfortunately
confused
promoted

1. You __________ me during your talk.
2. Jane's __________ toward her friend slowly changed.
3. __________, I could not find my missing watch.
4. Mr. Reynolds __________ Samantha to a better position.
5. The car cannot run without any __________ for the engine.

E Write the correct phrases in the blanks.

odd comment	write an essay	change careers
evaluate the results	mild weather	succeeds at

1. He wants to ______________ to become a teacher.
2. Everyone is enjoying the ______________ this spring.
3. He made an ______________ that surprised everyone.
4. Nancy often ______________ sporting events.
5. Let's ______________ of the online survey.
6. Please ______________ about your summer vacation.

F Circle the mistakes. Then, write the correct sentences.

1. Do you know when this milk will expiration?

➡ ______________________________

2. Please analysis this information and explain it to me.

➡ ______________________________

3. The clowns at the circus entertainment everyone last night.

➡ ______________________________

4. The company will expansion by opening several more stores.

➡ ______________________________

G Complete the crossword puzzle.

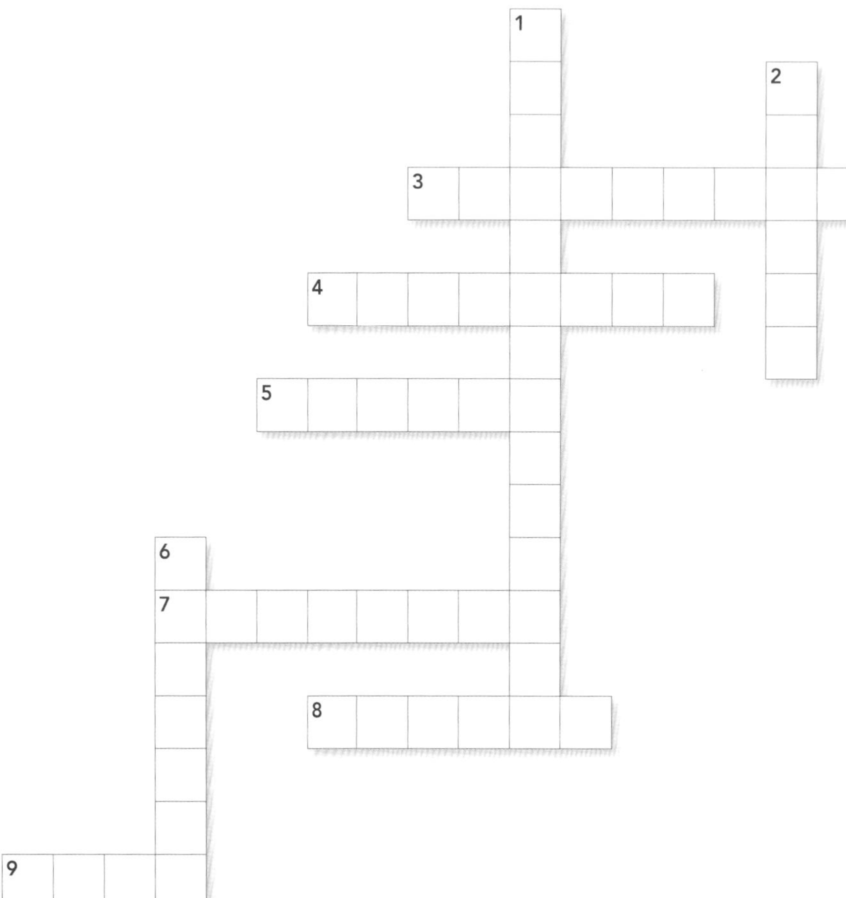

Across

3. existing for a long time

4. fragile or easily damaged

5. not proud or arrogant

7. to act on one another

8. a certain course of action

9. to give a person a job

Down

1. a personal feature or quality

2. a person younger than another

6. of different kinds or forms

H **Read the passage. Then, answer the questions below.**

Attending a University

Anna and Tim want to **acquire knowledge**. So they attend an **institute** of higher learning. Anna wants to become a **physician**. She learns about **genes**, **organs**, and other parts of the human body. Tim is interested in **economic** matters. He wants to learn about money, **imports**, and **statistics**.

They are **competitive**, so they sometimes take the same classes. Once, they take a **geology** class. They study **diverse** topics and learn about **rural** areas and unique **landscapes**.

Finally, they have at a big **ceremony** after finishing school. **Unfortunately**, Anna and Tim find jobs in different cities. They will have to **adjust** to life away from each other. They are **eager** to start their new lives. But they also think it will be **odd** not to see each other every day.

1. What is the passage mainly about?

a. different university classes people take

b. Anna's and Tim's time at a university

c. the reason people study at a university

d. the jobs Anna and Tim found

2. What does Anna want to be?

a. a geologist　　b. a physician

c. an economist　　d. a farmer

3. What do Anna and Tim do after they graduate?

a. go back to their homes　　b. become teachers

c. take a trip together　　d. get jobs in different cities

4. What does Tim want to learn about?

➡ ______________________________

5. What do Anna and Tim think will be odd?

➡ ______________________________

Unit 06 Word List

1 **accustom** [əkʌ́stəm]
v. to become familiar with through use
accustom oneself
→ I **accustomed** myself to living in a big city.

2 **appliance** [əpláiəns]
n. a piece of equipment used in the home
electric appliance
→ Ovens and refrigerators are electric **appliances**.

3 **basement** [béismənt]
n. a partly or completely underground floor in a building
in the basement
→ He keeps unused items in the **basement** at his home.

4 **boundary** [báundəri]
n. something that marks the farthest limits of an area (syn) border
mark a boundary
→ They will mark the **boundary** of their land.

5 **bulb** [bʌlb]
n. the glass case of an electric lamp
light bulb
→ I need to replace the light **bulb** in the kitchen.

6 **bush** [buʃ]
n. a low plant that has many branches
rose bush
→ She planted many rose **bushes** in her garden.

7 **chamber** [tʃéimbər]
n. a room in a house
private chamber
→ Nobody is allowed to enter his private **chamber**.

8 **feature** [fíːtʃər]
n. a characteristic that stands out (syn) character
main feature
→ Ed's main **features** are his bright blue eyes.

9 **install** [instɔ́ːl]
v. to connect or put where something can be used (ant) uninstall
install software
→ It is easy to **install** most software.

10 **ladder** [lǽdər]
n. wood or metal with two side pieces that people use to climb on
climb a ladder
→ You have to climb a **ladder** to get to the roof.

11 **obtain**
[əbtéin]
obtain - obtained - obtained

v. to get or acquire (ant) lose
obtain a job
→ He hopes to **obtain** a job this month.

12 **purchase**
[pə́:rtʃəs]
purchase - purchased - purchased

v. to buy (ant) sell
purchase groceries
→ She **purchases** groceries at the supermarket on Fridays.

13 **recently**
[rí:səntli]

adv. lately; a time not long ago (syn) nowadays
quite recently
→ Harry bought a new house quite **recently**.

14 **resident**
[rézidənt]

n. a person who lives in a certain place (syn) inhabitant
resident of
→ Chris is a **resident** of Paris.

15 **satisfy**
[sǽtisfài]
n. satisfaction

v. to gain one's needs or expectations (syn) please
satisfy one
→ The lunch really **satisfied** me.

16 **shelf**
[ʃelf]

n. a piece of wood, metal, etc. that is used to hold objects
on a shelf
→ Peter put some of his books on a **shelf**.

17 **shade**
[ʃeid]

n. a dark place where the sun's light is blocked (syn) shadow
in the shade
→ Let's stand in the **shade** where it is cool.

18 **slide**
[slaid]

v. to move down a smooth or slippery surface
n. a smooth surface that a person can move on
slide down → We will **slide** down the hill when it snows.
go down a slide → The children love to go down the **slide**.

19 **spectacular**
[spektǽkjələr]

adj. thrilling or impressive (syn) wonderful
spectacular display
→ The fireworks show was a **spectacular** display.

20 **surround**
[səráund]
surround - surrounded - surrounded

v. to be completely around something
surround ~ with
→ He **surrounded** his yard with a big fence.

Unit 06 Exercise

A Circle the words that fit the definitions.

1. the glass case of an electric lamp
   a. bulb　　b. feature　　c. shade　　d. slide
2. a piece of wood, metal, etc. that is used to hold objects
   a. basement　　b. bush　　c. shelf　　d. ladder
3. to gain one's needs or expectations
   a. accustom　　b. satisfy　　c. purchase　　d. install
4. a room in a house
   a. ladder　　b. slide　　c. resident　　d. chamber
5. a piece of equipment used in the home
   a. appliance　　b. bulb　　c. boundary　　d. basement

B Choose and write the correct words for the blanks.

obtain	purchase	resident	spectacular	install	boundary

1. wonderful = ____________
2. lose ≠ ____________
3. border = ____________
4. uninstall ≠ ____________
5. inhabitant = ____________
6. sell ≠ ____________

C Circle the words that best fit the sentences.

1. We used a slide | ladder to get to the top floor.
2. The tall trees create lots of shade | bulb for the yard.
3. Please tell me about the best bush | feature of this house.
4. Clara is accustomed | purchased to working hard every day.
5. The police surrounded | obtained the criminal and caught him.
6. The washing machine is downstairs in the shade | basement.

D Choose the correct words to complete the sentences.

1. ______________, the weather has been hot and sunny.
   a. Obtain b. Recently c. Surround d. Shade

2. The ______________ in front of the house is growing very high.
   a. slide b. ladder c. bush d. bulb

3. Many children play on a ______________ at the playground.
   a. shelf b. slide c. appliance d. chamber

4. The view of the Earth from outer space is ______________.
   a. recently b. resident c. feature d. spectacular

5. I hope to ______________ some food at the supermarket today.
   a. purchase b. surround c. install d. satisfy

E Read the passage. Then, fill in the blanks.

Lisa is a **resident** of an apartment building. **Recently**, she has wanted to move to a new home. She would like to **purchase** a house in the countryside. She looks at some ads and finds a **spectacular** house. It has several rooms, a swimming pool, and a large yard.

Lisa visits the house to check it out. When she arrives, she is pleased. There are many trees, so the yard gets plenty of **shade**. Then, she goes inside. The owner of the home recently **installed** some new **appliances** in the kitchen. So it looks nice. Lisa feels **satisfied** with that room. She checks out the other **chambers** and is also pleased. Finally, she goes down to the **basement**. Happy, Lisa decides to **purchase** the house at once.

1. Lisa wants to leave her apartment building and ______________ a house.

2. The ______________ house that Lisa looks at has a swimming pool.

3. The yard has ______________ because of all the trees.

4. There are many new ______________ in the kitchen.

Unit 07 Word List

1 **accompany** [əkʌ́mpəni]

v. to go together with (syn) escort

accompany somebody

→ I will **accompany** you to the airport.

2 **agency** [éidʒənsi]

n. a group or business that provides a service

travel agency

→ Joe bought his tickets through a travel **agency**.

3 **arise** [əráiz]

arise - arose - arisen

v. to wake up (syn) get up

arise at

→ Karen always **arises** at seven in the morning.

4 **comparison** [kəmpǽrisən]

v. compare

n. the act of saying how two things are the same or different (ant) contrast

in comparison

→ In **comparison**, the two countries are quite similar.

5 **delay** [diléi]

v. to put off until a later time

n. the act of putting off something until a later time

delay a flight → They will **delay** the flight until the snow stops falling.

long delay → We had a long **delay** at the train station.

6 **destination** [dèstənéiʃən]

n. the place where someone is going

final destination

→ His final **destination** is Tokyo, Japan.

7 **domestic** [dəméstik]

adj. relating to one's own country (ant) international

domestic travel

→ **Domestic** travel has been increasing lately.

8 **examine** [igzǽmin]

n. examination

v. to look at or study closely (syn) inspect

examine a painting

→ He is **examining** each painting carefully.

9 **extent** [ikstént]

n. the space or degree that something goes to

extent of

→ The **extent** of the country's land is the ocean.

10 **fluent** [flú(:)ənt]

adj. able to speak or write well or easily (syn) smooth

fluent speaker

→ June is a **fluent** speaker of English.

11 **frequent**
[frí:kwənt]
adv. frequently

adj. happening or taking place regularly (syn) common
frequent visitor
→ Mark is a **frequent** visitor at the city's museum.

12 **locate**
[lóukeit]
n. location

v. to find the place where something is
easily locate
→ She can easily **locate** places on maps.

13 **miserable**
[mízərəbl]

adj. very unhappy or uncomfortable
feel miserable
→ Tim felt **miserable** after eating the strange food.

14 **otherwise**
[ʌ́ðərwàiz]

conj. if not; or else
otherwise,
→ Be careful; **otherwise**, you may get in trouble.

15 **overseas**
[óuvərsì:z]

adv. across the sea (syn) abroad
adj. relating to travel across the sea
work overseas → Peter will work **overseas** for three years.
overseas vacation → They are planning to take an **overseas** vacation.

16 **prohibit**
[prouhíbit]

v. not to allow an activity (syn) ban (ant) permit
prohibit smoking
→ The city **prohibits** smoking in all restaurants.

17 **require**
[rikwáiər]
n. requirement

v. to need or demand
require money
→ Staying at a hotel **requires** money.

18 **sacred**
[séikrid]

adj. related to a religion (syn) holy
sacred book
→ The Bible is a **sacred** book in Christianity.

19 **somewhere**
[sʌ́mhwὲər]

adv. in an unknown place
somewhere else
→ They decided to eat **somewhere** else.

20 **wander**
[wɑ́ndər]

v. to move around with no goal or objective
wander around
→ Let's just **wander** around the city for a while.

Unit 07 Exercise

A Match the words with their definitions.

1. somewhere	•	• a. in an unknown place
2. locate	•	• b. to need or demand
3. delay	•	• c. very unhappy or uncomfortable
4. miserable	•	• d. to find the place where something is
5. frequent	•	• e. the place where someone is going
6. agency	•	• f. happening or taking place regularly
7. require	•	• g. to put off until a later time
8. destination	•	• h. a group or business that provides a service

B Circle the two words in each group that have the same meaning.

1. a. abroad	b. overseas	c. domestic	d. destination
2. a. locate	b. arise	c. get up	d. wander
3. a. frequent	b. ban	c. delay	d. prohibit
4. a. examine	b. inspect	c. comparison	d. accompany

C Circle the words that best fit the sentences.

1. Marcus is domestic | fluent in four languages.

2. Certain animals are overseas | sacred in some cultures.

3. What is the delay | extent of your scientific knowledge?

4. Three people will locate | accompany Susan on her trip.

5. John made a comparison | agency between the two cities.

6. Some people are wandering | prohibiting along the beach.

D Choose the correct words to complete the sentences.

1. Orville has been to most ______________ places of interest.
   a. miserable b. frequent c. domestic d. fluent

2. Please be quiet; ______________, you must leave the library.
   a. arise b. otherwise c. wander d. somewhere

3. People are ______________ from traveling to that island.
   a. prohibited b. examined c. located d. accompanied

4. John felt ______________ when he caught the flu.
   a. domestic b. miserable c. sacred d. overseas

5. Stephanie's final ______________ is the last stop for the train.
   a. extent b. agency c. destination d. comparison

E Read the passage. Then, write T for true or F for false.

Nowadays, people often travel **overseas**. They want to go **somewhere** they have never been. They are still making trips to **domestic** locations. But trips to other countries are more **frequent**.

First, each traveler **requires** a passport. **Otherwise**, that person cannot leave the country. Then, the person must make travel plans. Some people make reservations by themselves, but others use a travel **agency**. Lots of people think hard about their **destinations**. They **examine** lists of possible places to visit. Some only want to visit places where they are **fluent** in the language. Many people travel to **destinations** where they can **wander** around and visit **sacred** temples and other places. Problems may **arise** for them, but most of their trips are not **miserable**. Instead, those travelers have great times.

1. People are making frequent trips overseas. ______
2. All travelers use travel agencies. ______
3. Some people visit places only if they are fluent in the language. ______
4. Most people have miserable times on their trips. ______

Unit 08 Word List

1 **appropriate** [əpróupriət]
adj. right or okay for a certain purpose
appropriate clothes
→ Jim wore **appropriate** clothes for jogging.

2 **category** [kǽtəgɔ̀:ri]
n. a class of people, things, etc. that have similar characteristics
same category
→ These two sports belong to the same **category**.

3 **charity** [tʃǽrəti]
n. a group or organization that does work to help others
homeless charity
→ The homeless **charity** does good work in the city.

4 **clap** [klæp]
clap - clapped - clapped
v. to hit one's hands together to make a sound
clap loudly
→ They **clapped** loudly when the show ended.

5 **contribute** [kəntríbju:t]
n. contribution
v. to give money, time, etc. to help others (syn) donate
contribute to
→ Helen **contributes** to church each month.

6 **cooperate** [kouɑ́pərèit]
n. cooperation
v. to work together with another person
cooperate with
→ **Cooperate** with your teammates to win the game.

7 **deed** [di:d]
n. something that a person does (syn) act
good deed
→ Try to do five good **deeds** each day.

8 **devote** [divóut]
v. to spend time on a certain activity (syn) dedicate
devote time
→ Doug **devotes** time to solving puzzles.

9 **distribute** [distríbju(:)t]
n. distribution
v. to pass out or deliver something to others
distribute pamphlets
→ He **distributes** pamphlets for his club.

10 **earn** [ə:rn]
v. to gain something in return for working (syn) acquire
earn money
→ They **earn** money by working at a restaurant.

11 **garage** [gərάːdʒ]

n. a building or indoor area for parking vehicles in

one-car garage

→ Jason's house has a one-car **garage**.

12 **ingredient** [ingríːdiənt]

n. something that is one part of a mixture

cake ingredient

→ Flour, butter, and sugar are cake **ingredients**.

13 **needle** [níːdl]

n. a small, thin, pointed metal tool used for sewing

needle and thread

→ She can sew well with a **needle** and thread.

14 **occupy** [άkjəpài]

occupy - occupied - occupied

v. to take or fill up; to live in a place (syn) inhabit

occupy one's time → I **occupy** my time by reading books.

occupy a home → Greg **occupies** a home in the city.

15 **sculptor** [skʌ́lptər]

n. an artist who makes statues (syn) artist

famous sculptor

→ Michelangelo was a famous **sculptor**.

16 **sew** [sou]

v. to connect with stitches

sew a zipper

→ Please **sew** this zipper onto the jacket.

17 **subscribe** [səbskráib]

n. subscription

v. to pay to receive a newspaper, magazine, etc. on a regular basis

subscribe to

→ Mary **subscribes** to her local newspaper.

18 **trend** [trend]

n. an activity that is in style or popular

popular trend

→ Video games are a popular **trend** these days.

19 **viewer** [vjúːər]

v. view

n. a person who is watching something (syn) watcher

TV viewer

→ Millions of TV **viewers** watched the new program.

20 **whistle** [hwísl]

v. to make a musical sound by blowing out air between the teeth

whistle at

→ He **whistles** at his dogs to get them to come.

Unit 08 Exercise

A Circle the words that fit the definitions.

1. a small, thin, pointed metal tool used for sewing

a. charity　　b. needle　　c. sculptor　　d. trend

2. to pass out or deliver something to others

a. clap　　b. distribute　　c. sew　　d. occupy

3. a building or indoor area for parking vehicles in

a. category　　b. ingredient　　c. garage　　d. deed

4. something that a person does

a. deed　　b. category　　c. viewer　　d. charity

5. to spend time on a certain activity

a. earn　　b. cooperate　　c. subscribe　　d. devote

B Circle the two words in each group that have the same meaning.

1. a. donate　　b. needle　　c. sew　　d. contribute

2. a. subscribe　　b. viewer　　c. devote　　d. watcher

3. a. inhabit　　b. occupy　　c. deed　　d. whistle

4. a. garage　　b. cooperate　　c. acquire　　d. earn

C Circle the words that best fit the sentences.

1. People clap | earn for a performance if they like it.

2. Sue learned to sew | subscribe clothes from her mother.

3. John works for a deed | charity that tries to help people.

4. Please do not whistle | cooperate loudly inside the house.

5. What categories | ingredients are necessary to make cookies?

6. She is an excellent needle | sculptor and makes many statues.

D Choose the correct words to complete the sentences.

1. It is not ______________ to talk during a movie.

   a. viewer　　b. whistle　　c. appropriate　　d. earn

2. He ______________ to several magazines about sports.

   a. subscribes　　b. earns　　c. claps　　d. cooperates

3. Young children do not ______________ well with one another.

   a. cooperate　　b. sew　　c. distribute　　d. devote

4. Eric loves to follow new ______________ in pop culture.

   a. garages　　b. trends　　c. ingredients　　d. deeds

5. Put the various animals into the correct ______________.

   a. sculptors　　b. viewers　　c. needles　　d. categories

E Read the passage. Then, fill in the blanks.

Most people work or study several hours a day. When they finish, they have leisure time. They need something to do to **occupy** their leisure time. Some of these people do good **deeds**. For example, they **devote** a lot of time to working for **charities**. They might **distribute** food to the homeless. These people like to **contribute** to improving other people's lives.

Other people do different leisure activities. Some **subscribe** to magazines or newspapers and read them. Some people are **viewers** of TV programs and movies. One popular **trend** these days is **sewing**. Both men and women learn to **sew** clothes. It is a fun activity, and it teaches them to make their own clothes. They might even **earn** money by selling some of the clothes they make.

1. People may do good ______________ during their leisure time.

2. People who distribute food to the homeless ______________ to others' lives.

3. It is a popular trend for people to ______________ nowadays.

4. It is possible to ______________ money by selling clothes.

Unit 09 Word List

1 **afford**
[əfɔ́:rd]
adj. affordable

v. to have enough money to pay for
afford to
→ They can **afford** to take a family trip this year.

2 **anniversary**
[æ̀nəvə́:rsəri]

n. the yearly happening of a past event
wedding anniversary
→ Their wedding **anniversary** is on October 3.

3 **asset**
[ǽset]

n. something a person owns that has value
major asset
→ Most people's major **asset** is their home.

4 **bury**
[béri]
n. burial

v. to put in the ground and to cover with dirt
bury someone
→ We **buried** my grandfather in the cemetery.

5 **crawl**
[krɔ:l]

v. to move on one's hands and knees
crawl on
→ The baby is **crawling** on the floor.

6 **funeral**
[fjú:nərəl]

n. a ceremony for a dead person
have a funeral
→ They will have the **funeral** for Mr. Briggs tomorrow.

7 **grocery**
[gróusəri]

n. food and other items sold at a supermarket
grocery store
→ Jerry shops at the **grocery** store once a week.

8 **hospitality**
[hɑ̀spitǽləti]

n. the friendly greeting and treatment of guests (syn) friendliness
full of hospitality
→ They were full of **hospitality** toward their guests.

9 **immigrant**
[ímәgrənt]

n. a person who moves to live in another country (syn) settler
illegal immigrant
→ The illegal **immigrants** were sent back to their own country.

10 **individual**
[ìndəvídʒuəl]

n. a single person (syn) person, human
unique individual
→ Everyone on the Earth is a unique **individual**.

11 **lease**
[liːs]

v. to pay money to use land, a car, etc. (syn) rent
lease a car
→ Hailey **leased** a car for one year.

12 **neither**
[níːðər], [náiðər]

conj. not either of two people or things
neither ~ nor
→ She has **neither** a brother nor a sister.

13 **pregnant**
[prégnənt]

adj. having a child in one's body (syn) expecting
pregnant with
→ His mother is **pregnant** with twins.

14 **prosperity**
[prɑspérəti]

n. a successful condition (syn) wealth (ant) failure
peace and prosperity
→ This is a time of peace and **prosperity**.

15 **religious**
[rilídʒəs]
n. religion

adj. relating to a belief in a god or gods (syn) holy
religious belief
→ She can explain all of her **religious** beliefs.

16 **ritual**
[rítʃuəl]

n. an activity done for a religion or other purpose (syn) ceremony
birthday ritual
→ One common birthday **ritual** is giving gifts.

17 **sacrifice**
[sǽkrəfàis]

v. to give up one thing for another
sacrifice one's time
→ Keith **sacrifices** his free time for his family.

18 **significant**
[signífikənt]

adj. being important (ant) unimportant
significant job
→ Her mother has a **significant** job at a hospital.

19 **stove**
[stouv]

n. an appliance used for cooking (syn) oven, range
on a stove
→ Lisa is cooking spaghetti on a **stove**.

20 **struggle**
[strʌ́gl]
struggle - struggled - struggled

v. to try hard to do something
struggle to
→ Jeff **struggles** to pay his rent some months.

Unit 09 Exercise

A Circle the correct definitions for the given words.

1. a single person

a. grocery
b. stove
c. individual
d. anniversary

2. a ceremony for a dead person

a. immigrant
b. hospitality
c. ritual
d. funeral

3. to give up one thing for another

a. afford
b. struggle
c. lease
d. sacrifice

4. to put in the ground and to cover with dirt

a. bury
b. afford
c. crawl
d. struggle

B Write S for synonym or A for antonym next to each pair of words.

1. ________ friendliness – hospitality
2. ________ significant – unimportant
3. ________ pregnant – expecting
4. ________ failure – prosperity
5. ________ ritual – ceremony
6. ________ religious – holy

C Circle the words that best fit the sentences.

1. Joe can afford | bury to purchase a new house.

2. Let's boil some eggs on the anniversary | stove .

3. She sacrifices | struggles to do well in science class.

4. Martin is an asset | immigrant from another country.

5. It can be cheaper to lease | crawl a car than to buy one.

6. I need to buy some groceries | stoves to cook dinner.

D Choose the correct words to complete the sentences.

1. The company's ten-year ______________ is coming up next month.

a. prosperity b. anniversary c. ritual d. asset

2. Everyone watched the baby ______________ on the floor.

a. afford b. lease c. crawl d. sacrifice

3. I do not have time, and ______________ does Samantha.

a. stove b. religious c. neither d. significant

4. The bank has a lot of ______________ that it owns.

a. immigrants b. rituals c. individuals d. assets

5. We praised the host of the party for his ______________.

a. hospitality b. grocery c. funeral d. immigrant

E Read the passage. Then, write T for true or F for false.

Tim's family moved to a new country, so they are **immigrants**. At first, they **struggled** to do well in their new country. **Neither** his father nor his mother made a lot of money at their jobs. Then, Tim's mother got **pregnant**.

Tim's family could not **afford** to buy many **groceries**. They did not own a car either. They only **leased** one. Everyone **sacrificed** by giving up activities they enjoyed. Then, their neighbors started to help them. They realized that everyone in Tim's family was a good **individual**. Tim's father got a better job thanks to one neighbor. He made more money, so the family lived in **prosperity**. The baby was born on the second **anniversary** of their moving to their new country. It was a happy day for everyone.

1. Tim's family knew some immigrants from another country. ______

2. Tim's mother became pregnant. ______

3. Tim's family sacrificed by giving up certain activities. ______

4. Some neighbors helped Tim's family on their second anniversary. ______

Unit 10 Word List

1 **accurate** [ǽkjərit]
adj. having no errors (ant) wrong
accurate guess
→ Jane made an **accurate** guess about the problem.

2 **alien** [éiljən]
n. a being from outer space
alien invasion
→ **Alien** invasions are common in science-fiction films.

3 **awful** [ɔ́:fəl]
adj. very bad (syn) terrible (ant) terrific
awful performance
→ He gave an **awful** performance on the stage.

4 **brilliant** [bríljənt]
adj. very bright, talented, or intelligent
brilliant mind
→ Dave is a genius and has a **brilliant** mind.

5 **classify** [klǽsəfài]
n. classification
v. to put in different categories (syn) organize
classify books
→ Laura **classified** the books by their genres.

6 **concept** [kánsept]
n. an idea (syn) notion
have no concept
→ Patrick has no **concept** of time these days.

7 **desire** [dizáiər]
v. to want something very much
n. a strong feeling of wanting something (syn) wish
desire money → Lots of people **desire** money.
strong desire → Eric has a strong **desire** for a new house.

8 **distinguish** [distíŋgwiʃ]
v. to tell how something is different from another thing
distinguish between
→ Can you **distinguish** between the twin sisters?

9 **fit** [fit]
adj. appropriate or proper
fit for
→ This game is not **fit** for young children.

10 **mental** [méntəl]
adv. mentally
adj. relating to the mind (ant) physical
mental problem
→ Some people suffer from **mental** problems.

11 **motion**
[móuʃən]

n. the action of changing one's place or position
in motion
→ Soccer players are always in **motion**.

12 **objective**
[əbdʒéktiv]

n. something a person wants to do or accomplish (syn) goal
adj. not affected by personal feelings or opinions (ant) biased
final objective → The final **objective** of the game is to find the flag.
objective opinion → The judge wrote an **objective** opinion of the case.

13 **preference**
[préfərəns]
v. prefer

n. the act of liking one thing more than another
choose one's preference
→ Choose your **preference** from the menu.

14 **restore**
[ristɔ́:r]
n. restoration

v. to return something to its original condition
restore art
→ He **restores** art that is old and in bad condition.

15 **rush**
[rʌʃ]

v. to do an action fast (syn) hurry
rush around
→ They are **rushing** around and trying to clean the room.

16 **steady**
[stédi]

adj. even or regular in how one moves
steady walk
→ She goes around the lake at a **steady** walk.

17 **technique**
[tekní:k]

n. a method of doing something (syn) way
new technique
→ Jeff uses a new **technique** to lift weights.

18 **totally**
[tóutəli]
adj. total

adv. completely (syn) wholly
totally wrong
→ Your answer to the question was **totally** wrong.

19 **uncover**
[ʌnkʌ́vər]

v. to remove or show something (ant) conceal
uncover a clue
→ The players must **uncover** clues to solve the mystery.

20 **variety**
[vəráiəti]
adj. various

n. a number of different types of things
variety of
→ There are a **variety** of snacks to choose from.

Unit 10 Exercise

A Match the words with their definitions.

1. rush •
2. fit •
3. alien •
4. steady •
5. technique •
6. motion •
7. classify •
8. restore •

• a. even or regular in how one moves
• b. the action of changing one's place or position
• c. to do an action fast
• d. to return something to its original condition
• e. a being from outer space
• f. a method of doing something
• g. to put in different categories
• h. appropriate or proper

B Circle the two words in each group that are opposites.

1. a. objective	b. biased	c. concept	d. variety
2. a. restore	b. rush	c. uncover	d. conceal
3. a. dark	b. alien	c. brilliant	d. awful
4. a. distinguish	b. accurate	c. wrong	d. preference

C Circle the words that best fit the sentences.

1. The dinner tasted really steady | awful .

2. The idea is an interesting concept | variety .

2. Please state your clothing alien | preference .

4. We enjoy eating a desire | variety of different foods.

5. Getting enough sleep is good for your mental | objective health.

6. The farmer can distinguish | desire between all of the sheep in his flock.

D Choose the correct words to complete the sentences.

1. Julie has a ______________ to find a new job.

a. desire b. motion c. variety d. alien

2. George ______________ enjoyed the performance at the theater.

a. mental b. uncover c. brilliant d. totally

3. Please give an ______________ answer to each question.

a. steady b. brilliant c. accurate d. fit

4. Do you believe ______________ from other planets exist?

a. aliens b. objectives c. preferences d. desires

5. The man's ______________ is to finish school next year.

a. motion b. objective c. variety d. concept

E Read the passage. Then, fill in the blanks.

Playing games is popular these days. There are a **variety** of games to choose from. There are board games, video games, role-playing games, and many others. Usually, the **concept** of a game is simple. The **objective** should be clear because that makes people want to play it.

Some people have a **preference** for chess. It is **classified** as a **mental** game. The **objective** of the game is to capture the enemy's king. There are a **variety** of **techniques** people use when they play chess. Some of the most **brilliant** players **distinguish** themselves by winning lots of games. The best chess grandmasters can become world famous. Few people become grandmasters. But most people have a strong **desire** to play and to play well. So they improve at a **steady** rate.

1. A game usually has a simple ______________.

2. Chess is considered a ______________ game.

3. People use a ______________ of techniques to play chess.

4. Most people have a strong ______________ to play chess well.

Review 02 Units 06~10

A Choose and write the correct words for the definitions.

miserable	bury	hospitality	steady
alien	sculptor	boundary	fluent

1. even or regular in how one moves ➡ __________
2. very unhappy or uncomfortable ➡ __________
3. a being from outer space ➡ __________
4. able to speak or write well or easily ➡ __________
5. something that marks the farthest limits of an area ➡ __________
6. to put in the ground and to cover with dirt ➡ __________
7. the friendly greeting and treatment of guests ➡ __________
8. an artist who makes statues ➡ __________

B Circle the words that are the most similar to the underlined words.

1. Stella donates a lot of her free time to helping others.
   a. distributes b. contributes c. subscribes d. earns
2. There are few inhabitants in the city due to the typhoon.
   a. chambers b. shelves c. basements d. residents
3. John gave his seat on the bus to the expecting mother.
   a. pregnant b. significant c. religious d. brilliant
4. I try to get up around seven every morning.
   a. require b. accompany c. arise d. locate
5. We were surprised that his notion was the correct one.
   a. concept b. technique c. variety d. alien

C Choose the correct forms of the words to complete the sentences.

1. We were unable to location | locate the lost puppy.
2. It is clear that Angie has a mental | mentally problem.
3. The immigration | immigrant came from a county in Europe.
4. It will take a while to install | installation all of the equipment.
5. You will finish quickly if you cooperation | cooperate with each other.

D Complete the sentences with the words in the box.

1. The airline ______________ people from taking pets on flights.
2. My test score was ______________, so I failed the class.
3. She bought some new ______________ for her home.
4. Robert used the ______________ to make dinner last night.
5. Please behave in an ______________ manner at dinner.

awful
stove
appropriate
appliances
prohibits

E Write the correct phrases in the blanks.

desires money	clapped loudly	good deed
worked overseas	major asset	light bulb

1. Gold is a ______________________ for some investors.
2. Peter did a ______________________ by helping the old lady.
3. Thanks to the ______________________, we can see well at night.
4. Everyone ______________________ after Ryan scored a goal.
5. Karen ______________________ more than she wants happiness.
6. Susan ______________________ in South America for two years.

F Circle the mistakes. Then, write the correct sentences.

1. He goes to church weekly because of his religion beliefs.

   ➡ ______________________________

2. Alice is a frequently diner at that seafood restaurant.

   ➡ ______________________________

3. It will take years to restoration the old building that burned down.

   ➡ ______________________________

4. Please help her distribution those newspapers to everyone.

   ➡ ______________________________

5. John satisfaction his boss by doing a good job.

   ➡ ______________________________

G Complete the crossword puzzle.

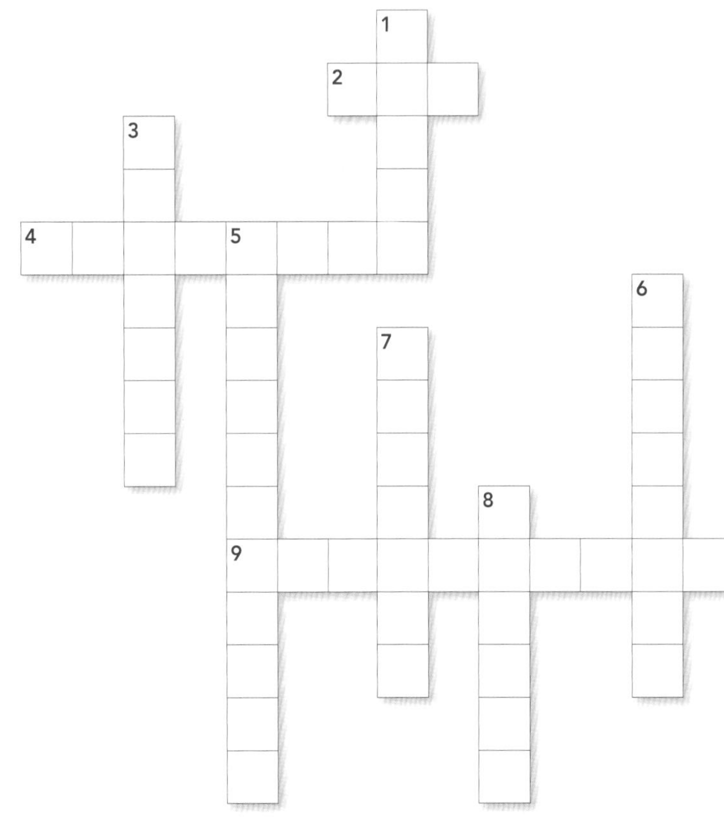

Across

2. to connect with stitches
4. to put in different categories
9. a single person

Down

1. to put off until a later time
3. a room in a house
5. being important
6. having no errors
7. to need or demand
8. a person who is watching something

H Read the passage. Then, answer the questions below.

The Hampton Family

The Hampton family members are **residents** of a small town. They **purchased** their home several years ago. At first, it was **surrounded** by weeds and looked **awful**. But they turned it into a **spectacular** place. Now, some of its **features** are fruit trees and rose **bushes**.

Mr. Hampton often works in his **garage**. He repairs **stoves** and other **appliances** in his free time. Mrs. Hampton is a **sculptor**. She also **sews** with a **needle** and thread. Her sewing **technique** is impressive. She has a **steady** hand and makes wonderful clothes.

Eric Hampton lives with his parents. But he is a **frequent** traveler **overseas**. He works at a travel **agency** and sometimes **accompanies** tourists. Tina Hampton is a quiet **individual**. She cannot **afford** to live alone, so she lives with her parents.

1. What is the passage mainly about?

a. the rooms in the Hampton family's home
b. the job that Mr. Hampton has
c. the lives of Eric and Tina Hampton
d. the work that the Hampton family members do

2. What is a feature of the Hampton family's home now?

a. lots of weeds
b. tall trees
c. fruit trees
d. a garden

3. What does Mrs. Hampton do?

a. She travels overseas.
b. She lives with her parents.
c. She sews with a needle and thread.
d. She repairs stoves and other appliances.

4. What does Mr. Hampton do in his free time?

➡ ______________________________

5. Why does Eric Hampton travel overseas?

➡ ______________________________

Unit 11 Word List

1 **advance** [ədvǽns]

v. to move forward (ant) retreat

advance toward

→ The army is **advancing** toward the enemy city.

2 **army** [á:rmi]

n. a large group of people trained to fight (syn) military

join the army

→ Tom joined the **army** after high school.

3 **conflict** [kánflikt]

n. a fight (syn) battle

win a conflict

→ The soldiers won the **conflict** in the morning.

4 **constant** [kánstənt]

adv. constantly

adj. continuing or not changing (syn) steady

constant fighting

→ There was **constant** fighting between the two sides.

5 **crew** [kru:]

n. the people who run a ship at sea or fly an aircraft

cabin crew

→ Julie was a member of the airline's cabin **crew**.

6 **crisis** [kráisəs]

n. a time when there is danger

economic crisis

→ The country is in the middle of an economic **crisis**.

7 **crush** [krʌʃ]

crush - crushed - crushed

v. to press or squeeze something to destroy it

crush a box

→ Steve **crushed** the box after he opened it.

8 **defeat** [difí:t]

defeat - defeated - defeated

v. to win against (syn) beat (ant) lose to

defeat someone

→ Irene **defeated** Mary in the tennis match.

9 **defend** [difénd]

v. to guard against an attack (syn) protect (ant) attack

defend against

→ They will **defend** the base against all attackers.

10 **facility** [fəsíləti]

n. something made to serve a specific function

medical facility

→ Many doctors work at the medical **facility**.

11 **identify**
[aidéntəfài]
n. identification

v. to recognize a certain person or thing
identify a person
→ He **identified** several people in the picture.

12 **leadership**
[líːdərʃìp]

n. the ability to guide or direct others (syn) management
strong leadership
→ John is known for his strong **leadership**.

13 **load**
[loud]

v. to put something on a vehicle
n. anything put on a vehicle to be transported
load a ship → They are **loading** the ship with boxes.
heavy load → The truck is carrying a heavy **load** of supplies.

14 **military**
[mílitèri]

n. the armed forces of a country (syn) army
adj. relating to war or being a soldier
advanced military → The United States has an advanced **military**.
military life → Harry quickly got used to **military** life.

15 **painful**
[péinfəl]

adj. causing a lot of hurt (syn) sore
painful injury
→ He went to the hospital for his **painful** injury.

16 **pursue**
[pərsjúː]
n. pursuit

v. to try to achieve something over a period of time
pursue a goal
→ Joe is **pursuing** his goal of becoming a doctor.

17 **revolution**
[rèvəljúːʃən]
adj. revolutionary

n. an attempt to change a government, often by fighting
American Revolution
→ The American **Revolution** ended in 1783.

18 **strategy**
[strǽtidʒi]

n. a plan or method of achieving a goal (syn) plan
new strategy
→ They used a new **strategy** to win the war.

19 **troop**
[truːp]

n. a group of soldiers (syn) army, military
armed troops
→ Armed **troops** are marching through the city.

20 **yield**
[jiːld]

v. to give up; to produce or harvest
yield to → We decided to **yield** to our opponents.
yield crops → The field **yielded** many crops this year.

Unit 11 Exercise

A Circle the words that fit the definitions.

1. a plan or method of achieving a goal

a. crew b. strategy c. army d. load

2. a time when there is danger

a. crisis b. troop c. military d. facility

3. to try to achieve something over a period of time

a. crush b. yield c. defend d. pursue

4. the armed forces of a country

a. conflict b. military c. leadership d. strategy

5. to put something on a vehicle

a. load b. identity c. defeat d. defend

B Write S for synonym or A for antonym next to each pair of words.

1. ________ defend – attack

2. ________ steady – constant

3. ________ sore – painful

4. ________ defeat – lose to

5. ________ advance – retreat

6. ________ management – leadership

C Circle the words that best fit the sentences.

1. This facility | crew is old and needs to be repaired.

2. A small troop | leadership of soldiers is on the base.

3. He believes he can yield | identify the thief to the police.

4. She took an orange and pursued | crushed it in her hands.

5. The army | crew is invading the country and attacking its cities.

6. The people rose up and started a military | revolution against the government.

D Choose the correct words to complete the sentences.

1. The ship's ________________ is sailing all the way to Europe.

a. crisis b. facility c. crew d. conflict

2. Harry joined the ________________ after he finished high school.

a. facility b. load c. strategy d. military

3. The wrestler ________________ and gave up the match.

a. pursued b. yielded c. defended d. loaded

4. Susan's ________________ worked and let her company make a lot of money.

a. strategy b. army c. troop d. load

5. The ________________ noise bothered everyone in the building.

a. constant b. military c. identify d. defend

E Read the passage. Then, write T for true or F for false.

Most countries have a **military**. They normally have an **army** with many **troops** as well as a navy with ships. The **crews** on the navy ships sail around their countries' waters. The soldiers in the **army defend** the country from danger.

When there is a **conflict** or **crisis**, **troops** may have to fight. First, the leaders of the **military** must **identify** the problem. Then, they come up with a **strategy**. They hope that their plan will let them **defeat** their enemies. If the army is fighting, it may **advance** in order to chase its enemies. Most armies try to **crush** their enemies and destroy the **facilities** of their enemies. They want to make fighting **painful** for their enemies. Doing that can let them win wars.

1. Most navy ships sail far from their home countries. ________

2. Troops may fight when there is a crisis. ________

3. Military leaders think of strategies to defeat their enemies. ________

4. Armies do not advance to chase their enemies. ________

Unit 12 Word List

No.	Word	Definition / Examples
1	**appeal** [əpíːl]	*v.* to ask for help or support *n.* a request for help or support appeal to → She **appealed** to the judge to let her go. make an appeal → The villagers made an **appeal** to the government.
2	**aspect** [ǽspekt]	*n.* one part of someone's or something's character unique aspect → Tom's unique **aspect** is his great intelligence.
3	**authority** [əθɔ́ːrəti]	*n.* power or the right to control others have authority → The government has **authority** over all of the citizens.
4	**cease** [siːs] cease - ceased - ceased	*v.* to stop doing something (ant) continue cease fighting → The general ordered the men to **cease** fighting.
5	**citizen** [sítizən]	*n.* a member of a nation or country citizen of → Ian is a **citizen** of England.
6	**complaint** [kəmpléint] *v.* complain	*n.* an expression of unhappiness, pain, regret, etc. (ant) praise major complaint → Our major **complaint** is that it is too expensive.
7	**copyright** [kápiràit]	*n.* the exclusive right to make copies of a creative work own a copyright → Keith owns the **copyright** to that song.
8	**criminal** [krímənəl]	*n.* a person guilty of a crime (syn) thief, robber *adj.* being guilty of breaking the law catch a criminal → The police hope to catch the **criminal**. criminal law → Erica is studying **criminal** law at school.
9	**debt** [det]	*n.* money that a person owes another person, bank, etc. (ant) asset have debt → He has **debt** from using his credit card.
10	**issue** [íʃuː]	*n.* something printed and given to others; a point of special importance latest issue → I have the latest **issue** of the magazine. difficult issue → The sickness is a difficult **issue** for people.

Unit 12

11 **lawyer** [lɔ́:jər]	*n.* a person who works in the field of law (syn) attorney work as a lawyer → Lee works as a **lawyer** in New York City.	
12 **legal** [lí:gəl]	*adj.* allowed or permitted by the law (ant) illegal legal act → The judge ruled that it was a **legal** act.	
13 **majority** [mədʒɔ́(:)rəti]	*n.* a number more than half of a total win a majority → Ellen won a **majority** of the votes and became president.	
14 **murder** [mə́:rdər]	*v.* to kill a person *n.* the act of killing a person murder someone → It is against the law to **murder** someone. commit murder → He went to jail for committing **murder**.	
15 **rob** [rɑb] *n.* robber	*v.* to take something without paying for it (syn) steal rob a bank → They **robbed** a bank and took a lot of money.	
16 **signature** [sígnətʃər]	*n.* a person's name written on paper (syn) autograph write one's signature → Paul wrote his **signature** on the contract.	
17 **suspect** *n.* [sʌ́spekt] *v.* [sʌspékt]	*n.* a person who is believed to have committed a crime *v.* to believe to be guilty, wrong, bad, etc. name a suspect → The police named a **suspect** in the crime. suspect of → She is **suspected** of stealing the money.	
18 **term** [tə:rm]	*n.* a period of time something lasts; a word or phrase used to name something single term → Harry served a single **term** as mayor. scientific term → This book has many scientific **terms** in it.	
19 **weapon** [wépən]	*n.* anything used in a fight with another person use a weapon → She used a **weapon** to defend herself.	
20 **witness** [wítnis] witness - witnessed - witnessed	*v.* to see by being at an event (syn) observe *n.* a person who sees something by being at an event witness a crime → Several people **witnessed** the crime. main witness → David was the main **witness** in the trial.	

Unit 12 Exercise

A Match the words with their definitions.

1. aspect
2. issue
3. term
4. legal
5. complaint
6. majority
7. suspect
8. authority

a. a number more than half of a total
b. one part of someone's or something's character
c. power or the right to control others
d. allowed or permitted by the law
e. to believe to be guilty, wrong, bad, etc.
f. an expression of unhappiness, pain, regret, etc.
g. a word or phrase used to name something
h. a point of special importance

B Circle the two words in each group that have the same meaning.

1. a. complaint	b. criminal	c. robber	d. suspect
2. a. autograph	b. appeal	c. legal	d. signature
3. a. attorney	b. lawyer	c. weapon	d. majority
4. a. murder	b. witness	c. rob	d. observe

C Circle the words that best fit the sentences.

1. I will rob | appeal to my manager and ask for help.

2. The man was a murder | witness to a robbery last night.

3. Every issue | citizen of the country must have an ID card.

4. Please appeal | cease causing so many problems for us.

5. Each soldier in the army is carrying a weapon | copyright .

6. You should pay back the aspect | debt as soon as possible.

D Choose the correct words to complete the sentences.

1. She wrote a novel and got the ______________ for it.
   a. citizen b. weapon c. copyright d. issue

2. Someone tried to ______________ the jewelry store last week.
   a. appeal b. rob c. murder d. witness

3. George hopes to become a ______________ in the future.
   a. debt b. majority c. weapon d. lawyer

4. Ellen was a ______________ to the car accident today.
   a. complaint b. witness c. lawyer d. issue

5. The police do not have any ______________ at this moment.
   a. authorities b. appeals c. suspects d. majorities

E Read the passage. Then, fill in the blanks.

All countries have laws. Laws control every **aspect** of society. They let **citizens** know which actions are **legal** and which are illegal. The **majority** of people are good **citizens** and follow the law. However, some people are **criminals**, so they break the law at times.

Some **criminals murder** others. This means that they kill people for no reason. **Criminals** might also **rob** people by stealing their possessions. When the **authorities** catch them, **criminals** get arrested. Then, they need a **lawyer**. The **lawyer** will defend them from any charges. If there is a court case, **witnesses** may speak for or against the **criminals**. If the **criminals** are guilty, they may have to serve a prison **term**. The length of the prison **term** depends on the illegal activity they did.

1. ______________ need to laws to know which actions are legal and illegal.

2. There are some ______________ that break the law.

3. ______________ happens when one person kills another.

4. Guilty criminals may have to serve a prison ______________.

Unit 13 Word List

1 **annoy**
[ənɔ́i]

v. to displease or trouble someone
annoy someone
→ David **annoyed** me with his singing.

2 **arrange**
[əréindʒ]
n. arrangement

v. to put in the proper place or order (syn) organize
arrange a room
→ I need to **arrange** the room now.

3 **claim**
[kleim]

v. to say that something is a fact (syn) announce
claim that
→ Sue **claimed** that she was telling the truth.

4 **combine**
[kəmbáin]
n. combination

v. to bring or put together (syn) connect (ant) separate
combine ingredients
→ **Combine** the ingredients and mix them together.

5 **comment**
[kɑ́ment]

v. to make a remark about something
n. a remark about something (syn) opinion
comment on → She **commented** on George's good manners.
make a comment → The president will make a **comment** soon.

6 **conduct**
n. [kɑ́ndʌ̀kt]
v. [kəndʌ́kt]

n. the way someone acts (syn) behavior
v. to behave in a certain way
good conduct → Mark praised the students for their good **conduct**.
conduct oneself → Please **conduct** yourself properly at the zoo.

7 **detect**
[ditékt]
detect - detected - detected

v. to discover something
detect a problem
→ Sara **detected** a problem in the report.

8 **doubt**
[daut]
adj. doubtful

v. to be uncertain about or not to believe (ant) believe
n. a feeling of uncertainty
doubt a story → Martina **doubted** Peter's story.
without a doubt → Without a **doubt**, we will win the game.

9 **exclaim**
[ikskléim]

v. to speak loudly or suddenly in surprise or anger (syn) shout
exclaim in
→ "What's that?" Todd **exclaimed** in surprise.

10 **highlight**
[háilàit]

n. the best or most memorable part of an event or time
highlight of
→ Visiting the palace was the **highlight** of our trip.

11 **including** [inklú:diŋ]

prep. together with

including some

→ Many people, **including** some movie stars, will attend the play.

12 **involve** [inválv]

v. to include or contain

involve steps

→ Solving the puzzle **involves** several steps.

13 **lately** [léitli]

adv. recently

do lately

→ What have you been doing **lately**?

14 **occur** [əkə́:r]

v. to take place (syn) happen

occur frequently

→ Rain **occurs** frequently during summer.

15 **recall** [rikɔ́:l]

v. to remember or bring back (ant) forget

recall one's name

→ Sorry, but I cannot **recall** your name.

16 **shut** [ʃʌt]

shut - shut - shut

v. to close

adj. closed (ant) open

shut a door → Always **shut** the door when you go out.

keep a window shut → Please keep the window **shut**.

17 **stare** [stɛər]

stare - stared - stared

v. to look at something very closely

stare at

→ The dog is **staring** at the cat.

18 **thirst** [θə:rst]

adj. thirsty

n. a desire to drink something

experience thirst

→ He experienced **thirst** while walking in the desert.

19 **tidy** [táidi]

adj. neat or orderly (ant) messy

tidy room

→ The little girl has a very **tidy** room.

20 **willing** [wíliŋ]

adj. wanting to do something (ant) unwilling

willing to

→ We are **willing** to follow your advice.

Unit 13 Exercise

A Circle the words that fit the definitions.

1. recently

   a. highlight　b. including　c. lately　d. thirst

2. to include or contain

   a. recall　b. involve　c. comment　d. occur

3. wanting to do something

   a. tidy　b. shut　c. willing　d. lately

5. to put in the proper place or order

   a. arrange　b. claim　c. annoy　d. stare

6. to speak loudly or suddenly in surprise or anger

   a. exclaim　b. detect　c. shut　d. conduct

B Choose and write the correct words for the blanks.

occur	comment	combine	doubt	recall	claim

1. believe ≠ ______________
2. happen = ______________
3. announce = ______________
4. separate ≠ ______________
5. opinion = ______________
6. forget ≠ ______________

C Circle the words that best fit the sentences.

1. I involved | shut the door and locked it.
2. It is rude to conduct | stare at other people.
3. Tell us about the thirst | highlight of your day.

4. Please stop annoying | commenting me with that music.
5. Sara embarrassed her parents with her poor conduct | doubt .
6. The students will make the classroom clean and willing | tidy .

D Choose the correct words to complete the sentences.

1. Nobody, ______________ the manager, could solve the problem.

a. including b. lately c. annoy d. doubt

2. Teresa experienced ______________ while running in the race.

a. comment b. thirst c. conduct d. highlight

3. The dog ______________ the missing person after the earthquake.

a. stared b. shut c. detected d. recalled

4. What will happen if you ______________ these two items?

a. annoy b. combine c. recall d. exclaim

5. I ______________ that anyone can finish the project on time.

a. arrange b. occur c. detect d. doubt

E Read the passage. Then, write T for true or F for false.

Every morning, Gina wakes up and makes her room **tidy**. She **arranges** everything in her room, **including** her clothes and books, to make it look nice. When she finishes, she **exclaims**, "That looks great." Then, Gina gets ready to go to work.

Gina works in an office all day long. Her work **involves conducting** research on different topics. The **highlight** of her day happens when she **detects** something interesting. That does not **occur** very often though. Sometimes her coworkers **annoy** her. They make problems, **including** talking too much and not **shutting** doors. If that happens, Gina cannot work, so she just **stares** at her computer screen. Fortunately, her coworkers do not **annoy** her very often. In fact, Gina cannot **recall** the last time that happened.

1. Gina makes her room tidy every evening. ________

2. Gina does research at her job. ________

3. Gina's coworkers are annoying her when they talk a lot. ________

4. When Gina's coworkers annoy her, she yells at them. ________

Unit 14 Word List

	Word	Definition / Examples
1	**ache** [eik]	*v.* to have constant pain *n.* a constant, dull pain ache badly → Amanda's tooth **aches** badly now. have an ache → I have a bad **ache** in my back.
2	**barely** [bέərli]	*adv.* in a way that almost does not happen (syn) scarcely barely survive → Several people **barely** survived the accident.
3	**burst** [bəːrst] burst - burst - burst	*v.* to break open suddenly burst into pieces → The vase **burst** into tiny pieces when he dropped it.
4	**caution** [kɔ́ːʃən] *adj.* cautious	*v.* to give a warning (syn) warn *n.* the act of paying attention in a dangerous situation caution someone → The doctor **cautioned** Mark not to eat junk food. use caution → You must use **caution** in certain situations.
5	**expose** [èkspóuz]	*v.* to lay open or uncover expose to → He was **exposed** to the sun for several hours.
6	**genuine** [dʒénjuin]	*adj.* real or original (ant) fake genuine diamond → Tom gave his wife a **genuine** diamond ring.
7	**heal** [hiːl]	*v.* to make healthy (syn) cure (ant) harm heal an injury → The medicine should **heal** your injury soon.
8	**highly** [háili]	*adv.* very much highly paid → The doctor is **highly** paid.
9	**identical** [aidéntikəl]	*adj.* alike in every way (ant) different identical twins → Mary and Beth are **identical** twins.
10	**injure** [índʒər] *n.* injury	*v.* to hurt or cause pain injure one's arm → Larry **injured** his arm while playing baseball.

Unit 14

11 **miracle** [mírəkl]

n. an event that does not happen naturally

real miracle

→ It was a real **miracle** that the patient stayed alive.

12 **modify** [mádəfài]

n. modification

v. to change something slightly

modify a car

→ He **modified** the car, so it goes fast

13 **outbreak** [áutbrèik]

n. a sudden start of something unpleasant

sudden outbreak

→ There was a sudden **outbreak** of the disease.

14 **reproduce** [rì:prədjú:s]

v. to make a copy; to produce young animals

reproduce pictures → The copier **reproduces** pictures very well.

reproduce quickly → Rabbits are animals that can **reproduce** quickly.

15 **rough** [rʌf]

adv. roughly

adj. having an uneven surface (ant) smooth

rough face

→ Eric has a **rough** face, so he needs to shave.

16 **scent** [sent]

n. a smell that is often pleasant (syn) odor

good scent

→ Many flowers have a good **scent**.

17 **sensitive** [sénsətiv]

adj. easily hurt or annoyed

sensitive person

→ He made that **sensitive** person cry with his comments.

18 **soul** [soul]

n. the spirit of a person that survives after death

human soul

→ He believes that humans' **souls** go to Heaven.

19 **suffer** [sʌ́fər]

v. to experience pain, difficulty, loss, etc. (ant) improve

suffer badly

→ John **suffered** badly from cancer.

20 **transform** [trænsfɔ́:rm]

n. transformation

v. to change in form or appearance (syn) change

transform into

→ A caterpillar can **transform** into a butterfly.

Unit 14 Exercise

A Circle the correct definitions for the given words.

1. highly

a. having an uneven surface
b. very much
c. easily hurt or annoyed
d. in a way that almost does not happen

2. soul

a. a constant, dull pain
b. an event that does not happen naturally
c. a smell that is often pleasant
d. the spirit of a person that survives after death

3. ache

a. to change something slightly
b. to make a copy
c. to change in form or appearance
d. to have constant pain

4. outbreak

a. a smell that is often pleasant
b. an event that does not happen naturally
c. a sudden start of something unpleasant
d. the act of paying attention in a dangerous situation

B Circle the two words in each group that are opposites.

1. a. ache b. fake c. burst d. genuine

2. a. improve b. suffer c. outbreak d. injure

3. a. harm b. sensitive c. soul d. heal

4. a. reproduce b. modify c. smooth d. rough

C Circle the words that best fit the sentences.

1. She blew up the balloon until it suffered | burst .

2. Anna reproduced | injured herself by falling off the ladder.

3. Chris needs to modify | heal the report to fix the mistakes.

4. He is so tired that he can highly | barely keep his eyes open.

5. The perfume Melinda is wearing has a nice scent | sensitive .

6. Many people believe that scents | miracles happen sometimes.

D Choose the correct words to complete the sentences.

1. The referee ______________ the players not to foul others.
   a. burst b. cautioned c. ached d. modified

2. The copy machine can ______________ all kinds of images.
   a. injure b. transform c. reproduce d. expose

3. Karen is ______________ and gets upset very easily.
   a. identical b. sensitive c. rough d. genuine

4. In the movie, the car can ______________ into a robot.
   a. transform b. modify c. injure d. ache

5. The policeman ______________ the criminals and arrested them.
   a. healed b. modified c. exposed d. burst

E Read the passage. Then, fill in the blanks.

In Mark's city, there is a sudden **outbreak**. Many people get sick with a disease. A lot of these people **suffer** from their sickness. One morning, Mark wakes up and feels ill. His symptoms are **identical** to the ones other people have.

Mark immediately goes to the doctor. The doctor tells Mark it is **highly** likely that he is sick. He **cautions** Mark to stay home. That way, Mark will not **expose** other people to the sickness. Mark's body **aches**. He can **barely** breathe. He has a **rough** time for several days. He experiences **genuine** fear because he believes his body might not **heal**. Slowly, however, Mark gets better. After a few days, he is no longer sick. Mark says it is a **miracle** that he is better.

1. There is an ______________ of a disease in Mark's city.
2. Mark's symptoms are ______________ to those of other people.
3. Mark's body aches, and he can ______________ breathe.
4. It is a ______________ when Mark gets better.

Unit 15 Word List

1 **account** [əkáunt]
n. an amount of money kept in a bank
v. to give an explanation
savings account → She put some money in her savings **account**.
account for → Can you **account** for the missing item?

2 **approach** [əpróutʃ]
v. to go near or toward
approach someone
→ My boss **approached** me after lunch.

3 **circumstance** [sə́ːrkəmstæ̀ns]
n. a condition or detail that affects something else (syn) situation
changing circumstances
→ George canceled his trip due to changing **circumstances**.

4 **client** [kláiənt]
n. a person who gets advice from a professional
regular client
→ John is a regular **client** of this company.

5 **conference** [kánfərəns]
n. a meeting to discuss something (syn) forum
have a conference
→ The men are having a **conference** right now.

6 **credit** [krédit]
n. a good reputation that lets a person borrow money
good credit
→ Susan has good **credit** at her bank.

7 **currency** [kə́ːrənsi]
n. money (syn) cash
exchange currency
→ You can exchange **currency** at the airport.

8 **deposit** [dipázit]
v. to put somewhere safe, such as in a bank (ant) withdraw
deposit money
→ I **deposit** money in the bank once a month.

9 **dispute** [dispjúːt]
v. to argue or debate
n. an argument between two or more people
dispute a matter → They are **disputing** a matter in Mr. Lee's office.
have a dispute → The men have a **dispute** about the contract.

10 **duty** [djúːti]
n. something one is expected or has to do
do one's duty
→ You should always do your **duty**.

11 **enterprise**
[éntərpràiz]

n. a project or business
small enterprise
→ My aunt runs a small **enterprise** in the city.

12 **export**
v. [ikspɔ́ːrt]
n. [ékspɔːrt]

v. to send goods to other countries to sell (ant) import
n. the act of sending goods to another country to sell
export goods → Korea **exports** goods to many countries.
major export → Oil is a major **export** of Saudi Arabia.

13 **industry**
[índəstri]
adj. industrial

n. any kind of business activity
tourist industry
→ The tourist **industry** makes a lot of money each year.

14 **labor**
[léibər]

v. to do work
n. work a person does
labor at → Tom **labored** at his job all day long.
hard labor → He did hard **labor** for several hours.

15 **merchant**
[məːrtʃənt]

n. a person who buys and sells goods (syn) trader
gold merchant
→ Lisa bought the ring from a gold **merchant**.

16 **propose**
[prəpóuz]
n. proposal

v. to offer or suggest (syn) recommend
propose an idea
→ I **proposed** an idea that my boss liked.

17 **quantity**
[kwántəti]

n. an amount of something
large quantity
→ The man bought a large **quantity** of paper.

18 **stamp**
[stæmp]

v. to put a mark on
stamp a document
→ The secretary **stamped** a document in the office.

19 **translate**
[trænsléit]
n. translation

v. to change from one language to another (syn) interpret
translate from
→ Isabella can **translate** from French to Italian.

20 **utilize**
[júːtəlàiz]

v. to put to use
utilize for
→ He will **utilize** the computer for his job.

Unit 15 Exercise

A Match the words with their definitions.

1. labor	a. work a person does
2. account	b. something one is expected or has to do
3. stamp	c. any kind of business activity
4. industry	d. a project or business
5. currency	e. to put a mark on
6. enterprise	f. a good reputation that lets a person borrow money
7. credit	g. an amount of money kept in a bank
8. duty	h. money

B Choose and write the correct words for the blanks.

deposit conference circumstance propose translate export

1. situation = ____________
2. withdraw ≠ ____________
3. interpret = ____________
4. recommend = ____________
5. import ≠ ____________
6. forum = ____________

C Circle the words that best fit the sentences.

1. You should not propose | approach a growling dog.
2. Many people utilize | deposit computers to do work.
3. The labor | merchant offered the customer a good price.
4. The client | credit will arrive at the airport in a few hours.
5. There is only a small quantity | duty of sugar in the container.
6. She got in a credit | dispute with her mother about her homework.

D Choose the correct words to complete the sentences.

1. You must get foreign ______________ when you travel abroad.
   a. deposit b. client c. merchant d. currency

2. All the workers do their ______________ every day.
   a. enterprise b. export c. dispute d. duty

3. We must find someone to ______________ these papers.
   a. account b. translate c. approach d. propose

4. Todd ______________ going on a picnic this weekend.
   a. utilized b. proposed c. deposited d. labored

5. Many people are attending the ______________ on robotics.
   a. conference b. merchant c. industry d. quantity

E Read the passage. Then, write T for true or F for false.

Peter is a **merchant**. He has his own store and has many **clients**. One day, he decides to start **exporting** goods to other countries. He has a **conference** with his partner and **proposes** an idea. His partner agrees, so they think about how they will **approach** this new plan.

Peter and his partner establish an **enterprise** in another country. It is a business in the manufacturing **industry**. They open an **account** at a bank and **deposit** money in it. Then, they hire some workers and tell them about their **duties**. The workers speak a different language, so Peter must **translate** everything he says. The work goes well, and the business gets many new clients. Peter has some **disputes** with these **clients**, but he usually solves those problems quickly.

1. Peter is the client of a merchant. ______
2. Peter's partner is from another country. ______
3. Peter's business is in manufacturing. ______
4. The business gets many new clients. ______

Review 03 Units 11~15

A Choose and write the correct words for the definitions.

comment	expose	yield	murder
enterprise	crush	authority	dispute

1. to make a remark about something ➡ ______________
2. to press or squeeze something to destroy it ➡ ______________
3. an argument between two or more people ➡ ______________
4. power or the right to control others ➡ ______________
5. to lay open or uncover ➡ ______________
6. a project or business ➡ ______________
7. the act of killing a person ➡ ______________
8. to surrender or give up ➡ ______________

B Circle the words that are the most similar to the underlined words.

1. Everyone is very disappointed with Jeff's <u>behavior</u>.
   a. thirst   b. doubt   c. conduct   d. highlight

2. Susan <u>recommends</u> that we have dinner at a restaurant tonight.
   a. approaches   b. proposes   c. translates   d. exports

3. Greg's broken arm is very <u>sore</u> right now.
   a. military   b. constant   c. criminal   d. painful

4. The <u>thief</u> stole some money from the bank.
   a. criminal   b. citizen   c. witness   d. suspect

5. There is a pleasant <u>odor</u> coming from the kitchen.
   a. soul   b. scent   c. outbreak   d. caution

C Choose the correct forms of the words to complete the sentences.

1. I doubtful | doubt that the story you told is true.
2. Please identify | identification yourself before you speak.
3. Everyone here is a citizen | citizenship of another country.
4. The surface feels roughly | rough and needs to be smooth.
5. Some people know how to translation | translate that language.

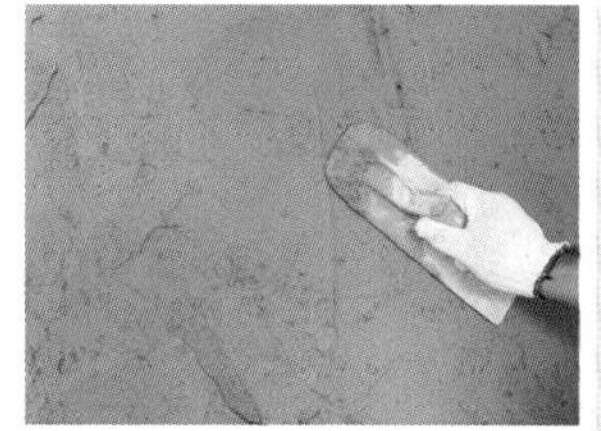

D Complete the sentences with the words in the box.

1. It is polite to ______________ the door after you leave.
2. Several ______________ wanted to meet Ms. Smith today.
3. The ______________ of that book will end in a few years.
4. He is ______________ a lot because of his illness.
5. The general's ______________ helped him win the war.

shut
suffering
leadership
copyright
clients

E Write the correct phrases in the blanks.

have a conference	highly paid	tidy room
rob a bank	identical twins	joined the army

1. Pro soccer players are very ______________________.
2. Irene's two brothers are ______________________.
3. He will ______________________ since he has no money.
4. His parents want him to have a ______________________.
5. Chris ______________________ and became a soldier.
6. We will ______________________ as soon as lunch ends.

F Circle the mistakes. Then, write the correct sentences.

1. Let's combination everything and mix it together.

➡ ______________________________

2. We must defense our country from the enemy.

➡ ______________________________

3. I cautious her to be careful on her trip last week.

➡ ______________________________

4. Mr. Kennedy has a job in the computer industrial.

➡ ______________________________

5. Ken filed a complain about his neighbor to the landlord.

➡ ______________________________

G Complete the crossword puzzle.

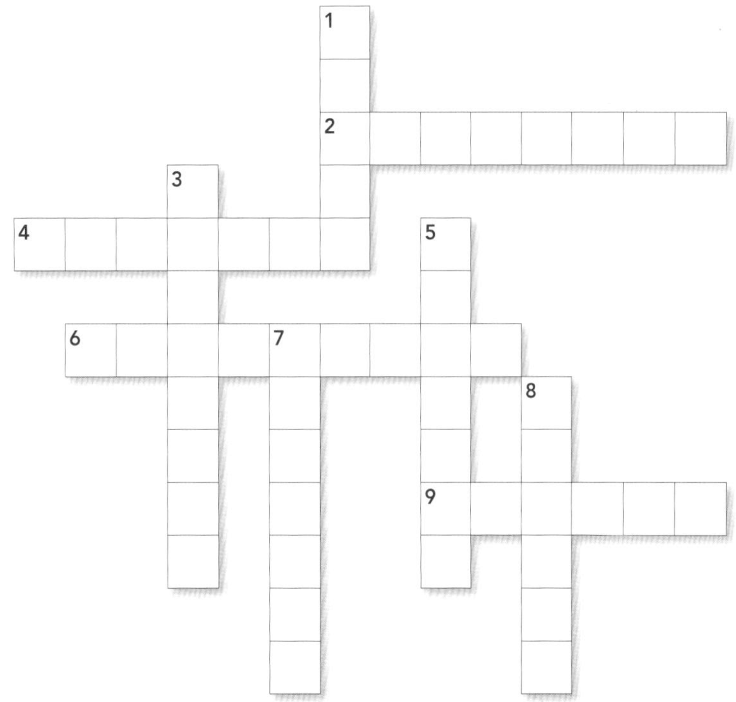

Across

2. to go near or toward
4. real or original
6. easily hurt or annoyed
9. a time when there is danger

Down

1. to stop doing something
3. an amount of something
5. to move forward
7. to include or contain
8. a desire to drink something

H Read the passage. Then, answer the questions below.

The News

Every night, Mary watches the news on television. Tonight, the **highlights** on the news **annoy** her. First, the **outbreak** of a virus is **occurring** in her country. The government is **cautioning** people to be careful. The **highly painful** virus makes people **suffer** and their bodies **ache**, and doctors are trying to **heal** sick patients.

Another news report is about a **legal dispute** between some **merchants**. They are in the computer **industry** and are trying to **export** goods to other countries. She thinks that their behavior is **criminal**. She believes they are **robbing** people. There is also a report about a **citizen** who **murdered** someone. Finally, the news reports that the **army** in another country is **crushing** a **revolution**. She thinks it is a serious **crisis**.

1. What is the passage mainly about?

a. an illness
b. some news reports
c. Mary's feelings
d. a revolution

2. What is the government cautioning people about?

a. a virus
b. a revolution
c. a merchant
d. a criminal

3. What does Mary think about the merchants?

a. They are murderers.
b. They are dangerous.
c. They are criminals.
d. They are good people.

4. What does the virus do to people?

➡ ______________________________

5. What is the army in another country doing?

➡ ______________________________

Unit 16 Word List

1 **acknowledge** [əknɑ́lidʒ]

v. to say that something is real or true

acknowledge one's mistake

→ Terry **acknowledged** his mistakes to Jane.

2 **admit** [ədmít]

n. admission

v. to allow to enter (syn) let in

admit to

→ They were **admitted** to the amusement park.

3 **belong** [bilɔ́(:)ŋ]

v. to be a member of; to be the property of (syn) own

belong in → You do not **belong** in this group.

belong to → This bicycle **belongs** to Greg.

4 **bond** [bɑnd]

n. something that binds or holds people or things together

strong bond

→ They built a strong **bond** with their coach.

5 **charm** [tʃɑːrm]

adj. charming

v. to delight or please through beauty, good manners, etc.

n. the power to delight or please

be charmed → Everyone was **charmed** by the movie star's good looks.

a lot of charm → Helen is popular as she has a lot of **charm**.

6 **compassion** [kəmpǽʃən]

n. a feeling of pity for someone experiencing something bad

feel compassion

→ We felt **compassion** toward the sick man.

7 **contrast** [kɑ́ntræst]

v. to say how two people or things are different (ant) compare

n. the act of saying how two people or things are different

contrast ~ with → Please **contrast** apples with oranges.

in contrast → In **contrast** to summer, winter is very cold.

8 **deliberate** [delíbərit]

adj. carefully considered; planned or on purpose

deliberate decision → After talking, they made a **deliberate** decision.

quite deliberate → Tom's speech was quite **deliberate**.

9 **envy** [énvi]

adj. envious

n. a feeling of unhappiness toward another person's success (syn) jealousy

feel envy

→ I felt **envy** toward John when he won the lottery.

10 **exaggerate** [igzǽdʒərèit]

v. to say that something is greater than reality

exaggerate facts

→ Do not **exaggerate** the facts when you speak.

11 **guarantee** [gærəntíː]

v. to promise to do something in the future (syn) promise
n. a promise that a person will do something
guarantee to → The company **guarantees** to replace any broken items.
make a guarantee → The boy made a **guarantee** to his parents.

12 **honor** [ánər]

n. honesty and fairness in one's beliefs and actions
man of honor
→ Mr. Thompson is a man of **honor**.

13 **illegal** [ilíːgəl]

adj. against the law (syn) wrong (ant) legal
illegal action
→ Lewis was arrested for his **illegal** actions.

14 **intend** [inténd]
n. intention

v. to plan or design something for a purpose
intend to
→ We **intend** to take a trip this weekend.

15 **interrupt** [ìntərʌ́pt]
n. interruption

v. to stop a person in the middle of doing something
interrupt someone
→ Do not **interrupt** me when I am on the phone.

16 **laughter** [lǽftər]
v. laugh

n. a sound that shows amusement
loud laughter
→ Loud **laughter** came from the theater.

17 **pause** [pɔːz]

v. to make a short stop
n. a short stop (syn) break
pause for → Paula **paused** for a minute and then continued talking.
long pause → There was a long **pause** between the question and the answer.

18 **ponder** [pándər]

v. to think about something deeply (syn) consider
ponder over
→ Carl **pondered** over his future last night.

19 **tempt** [tempt]
n. temptation

v. to attract or appeal to strongly
tempt someone
→ The money **tempted** me to enter the contest.

20 **voluntary** [váləntèri]
n., v. volunteer

adj. done or made by one's own decision (ant) unwilling
voluntary donation
→ I made a **voluntary** donation to the homeless shelter.

Unit 16 Exercise

A Circle the correct definitions for the given words.

1. ponder
   a. to plan or design something for a purpose
   b. to think about something deeply
   c. to promise to do something in the future
   d. to say how two people or things are different

2. interrupt
   a. to be the property of
   b. to say that something is greater than reality
   c. to attract or appeal to strongly
   d. to stop a person in the middle of doing something

3. belong
   a. to be a member of
   b. to say how two people or things are different
   c. to attract or appeal strongly
   d. to delight or please through beauty, good manners, etc.

4. charm
   a. the power to delight or please
   b. something that binds or holds people or things together
   c. honesty and fairness in one's beliefs and actions
   d. a feeling of pity for someone experiencing something bad

B Circle the two words in each group that have the same meaning.

1. a. break	b. pause	c. contrast	d. charm
2. a. admit	b. let in	c. ponder	d. interrupt
3. a. voluntary	b. honor	c. jealousy	d. envy
4. a. compassion	b. promise	c. acknowledge	d. guarantee

C Circle the words that best fit the sentences.

1. It is illegal | voluntary to steal from other people.
2. I contrast | acknowledge that this is the best solution.
3. The smell of the chocolate tempted | contrasted us to eat it.
4. He always acts with laughter | honor in everything he does.
5. The nurse showed compassion | laughter to the sick patient.

D Choose the correct words to complete the sentences.

1. Attendance at the meeting this weekend is ________________.
   a. deliberate b. illegal c. laughter d. voluntary

2. People often ________________ the truth when they tell stories.
   a. admit b. exaggerate c. contrast d. guarantee

3. We could hear ________________ coming from the classroom.
   a. honor b. envy c. pause d. laughter

4. The man and his dog have a strong ________________ with each other.
   a. bond b. guarantee c. contrast d. pause

5. Irene ________________ to find a new job next month.
   a. acknowledges b. intends c. charms d. belongs

E Read the passage. Then, fill in the blanks.

Everyone has friends. People like to connect with one another. This is a **deliberate** action by them. They **acknowledge** that having friends can improve the quality of their lives. Plus, **voluntary** friendships can benefit both people. People can learn from one another just by being friends.

It is not always easy to have friends though. Many people **admit** that it can be difficult. For example, some friends **interrupt** others while they are talking. They do not **intend** to annoy their friends, yet people do not like that. In addition, some people **envy** the success of their friends. They might get jealous if one of their friends is successful or does something well. Still, most friendships are filled with **laughter**. So people enjoy spending time with one another.

1. It is ________________ for people to try to connect with one another.

2. ________________ friendships are able to help both people.

3. People who interrupt others do not ________________ to annoy them.

4. Friendships often have a lot of ________________ since people like their friends.

Unit 17 Word List

1 **according** [əkɔ́ːrdiŋ]

adj. as said by
according to
→ **According** to the president, the war is almost over.

2 **archaeology** [ɑ̀ːrkiɑ́lədʒi]
n. archaeologist

n. the study of prehistoric people and their cultures
Egyptian archaeology
→ Sue plans to study Egyptian **archaeology** at school.

3 **biography** [baiɑ́grəfi]

n. a written work about a person's life
read a biography
→ He is reading a **biography** of Julius Caesar.

4 **canal** [kənǽl]

n. an artificial waterway connecting two bodies of water
build a canal
→ It took many years to build the Panama **Canal**.

5 **civilization** [sìvəlizéiʃən]

n. a state in human society with a high degree of culture
ancient civilization
→ The Mesopotamians founded an ancient **civilization**.

6 **decade** [dékeid]

n. a period lasting ten years
for a decade
→ She lived in Japan for a **decade** or so.

7 **disaster** [dizǽstər]

n. a terrible event in which many people may be killed (syn) tragedy
major disaster
→ The earthquake caused a major **disaster**.

8 **eruption** [irʌ́pʃən]

n. a sudden and violent explosion
volcanic eruption
→ The volcanic **eruption** caused a deadly tsunami.

9 **fame** [feim]
adj. famous

n. a widespread reputation, particularly one that is positive
achieve fame
→ Glen achieved **fame** for becoming the country's president.

10 **instance** [ínstəns]

n. the case of something (syn) example
for instance
→ For **instance**, Isaac Newton was a famous scientist.

11 **masterpiece** [mǽstərpis]

n. a person's greatest work of art

create a masterpiece

→ Michelangelo created a **masterpiece** when he made the statue *David*.

12 **meteor** [mí:tiər]

n. a small rock or dust that enters the Earth's atmosphere

see a meteor

→ If you see a **meteor**, it will move fast in the sky.

13 **obvious** [ɑ́bviəs]
adv. obviously

adj. easily seen or understood (syn) clear (ant) hidden

be obvious

→ The best president in the country's history is **obvious**.

14 **patent** [pǽtənt]

n. the right to make, use, or sell an invention
v. to get the exclusive rights to an invention

file a patent → The inventor filed a **patent** on his machine.
patent something → She plans to **patent** her latest invention.

15 **priest** [pri:st]

n. a person who performs religious duties (syn) pastor

become a priest

→ John decided to become a **priest** late in life.

16 **random** [rǽndəm]

adj. happening without reason or pattern (syn) accidental

random event

→ Sometimes a **random** event can change history.

17 **rescue** [réskju:]

v. to save a person from a dangerous situation

rescue someone

→ The firefighters **rescued** several people from the building.

18 **severe** [sivíər]
adv. severely

adj. harsh or very serious (ant) easygoing

severe penalty

→ There is a **severe** penalty for liars.

19 **tension** [ténʃən]

n. mental or emotional stress

a lot of tension

→ There is a lot of **tension** because of the election.

20 **urban** [ə́:rbən]

adj. relating to a city (ant) rural

urban environment

→ Craig prefers to live in an **urban** environment these days.

Unit 17 Exercise

A Circle the words that fit the definitions.

1. a widespread reputation, particularly one that is positive

a. fame　b. disaster　c. patent　d. meteor

2. mental or emotional stress

a. masterpiece　b. archaeology　c. instance　d. tension

3. as said by

a. urban　b. according　c. severe　d. obvious

4. a period lasting ten years

a. eruption　b. canal　c. decade　d. civilization

5. a sudden and violent explosion

a. eruption　b. tension　c. priest　d. biography

B Write S for synonym or A for antonym next to each pair of words.

1. ________ hidden – obvious　**2.** ________ instance – example

3. ________ urban – rural　**4.** ________ accidental – random

5. ________ pastor – priest　**6.** ________ severe – easygoing

C Circle the words that best fit the sentences.

1. She wrote a biography | meteor about her father.

2. We must rescue | disaster the people in the accident.

3. The disaster | meteor appeared in the sky late at night.

4. He will patent | rescue his invention to make money from it.

5. There was a civilization | patent in Egypt thousands of years ago.

6. I learned a lot about ancient random | archaeology by reading books.

D Choose the correct words to complete the sentences.

1. They built a ______________ to connect the two rivers.
   a. decade b. canal c. biography d. patent

2. She considers this painting to be her ______________.
   a. instance b. masterpiece c. priest d. patent

3. The collapse of the bridge was a big ______________.
   a. disaster b. meteor c. civilization d. tension

4. Many people in ______________ centers live in apartments.
   a. severe b. random c. obvious d. urban

5. Doug suffered a ______________ injury during a baseball game.
   a. according b. urban c. instance d. severe

E Read the passage. Then, write T for true or F for false.

When Helen was young, she read many books. She especially loved **biographies**. She read all about famous people from the past. So she decided to study history when she went to college. She wanted to learn about ancient **civilizations**.

One class she took was about ancient Egypt. **According** to her professor, the Egyptians had a very advanced society. Many people were farmers, but there were also some **urban** centers. The Egyptians had **priests** at their temples. They also built **canals** to help move the water in the Nile River to their farms. Helen believes it is **obvious** that the Egyptians were very smart. She thinks the Egyptians earned their fame for their civilization. She decides to take an **archaeology** class to learn more about them.

1. Helen read many biographies about famous people. ________
2. The Egyptians did not have any urban centers. ________
3. There were canals during the time of ancient Egypt. ________
4. Helen does not want to take any archaeology classes. ________

Unit 18 Word List

1 **aid** [eid]

v. to provide support or help (syn) assist
n. support or help, such as money, food, or advice
aid someone → Please **aid** me with my homework.
provide aid → The police provided **aid** for the homeowners.

2 **assembly** [asémbli]

n. the coming together of people for a purpose (syn) meeting
school assembly
→ All the students got together for the school **assembly**.

3 **candidate** [kǽndidèit]

n. a person who is trying to win an office, job, award, etc.
presidential candidate
→ There are three presidential **candidates** this year.

4 **congress** [káŋgrəs]

n. a large meeting held to discuss ideas or policies
have a congress
→ They will have a **congress** to talk about the problems.

5 **convince** [kənvíns]

v. to persuade a person to one's opinion
convince somebody
→ Janet **convinced** everyone by making a good argument.

6 **corrupt** [kərʌ́pt]
n. corruption

adj. being evil or lacking honesty (ant) moral
corrupt politician
→ The **corrupt** politician was sentenced to prison.

7 **democracy** [dimákrəsi]

n. a type of government in which people can vote
live in a democracy
→ Many people live in **democracies**.

8 **demonstrate** [démənstrèit]

v. to prove; to march to show one's opinion
demonstrate that → Rachel **demonstrated** that her idea was correct.
demonstrate against → The group is **demonstrating** against the president.

9 **establish** [istǽbliʃ]

v. to create or start (syn) found
establish a restaurant
→ John **established** a restaurant in 2020.

10 **forbid** [fərbíd]

v. to prohibit or make a law against something (ant) allow
forbid ~ from
→ The government **forbids** people from owning guns.

11 **govern** [gʌ́vərn]

v. to rule over others

govern a country

→ She **governed** a country for four years.

12 **license** [láisəns]

n. an agreement from a government to do something (syn) permit

driver's license

→ Greg bought a car since he has a **driver's license**.

13 **negative** [négətiv]

adj. refusing to allow or do something (ant) positive

negative response

→ Karen gave a **negative** answer to my request.

14 **political** [pəlítikəl]

n. politics

adj. relating to the act of ruling or governing

political act

→ Everything the president does is a **political** act.

15 **prejudice** [prédʒədis]

n. a negative feeling based on emotion rather than fact

form of prejudice

→ Racism is a form of **prejudice**.

16 **principal** [prínsəpəl]

adj. first in rank, importance, etc. (syn) chief (ant) least

principal reason

→ What is the **principal** reason you are moving?

17 **reverse** [rivə́:rs]

adj. opposite in method, direction, order, etc.

reverse direction

→ Let's turn around and go in the **reverse** direction.

18 **state** [steit]

n. statement

n. the condition of a person or thing

v. to say something

in a state → Peter is in a **state** of good health.

state that → The man **stated** that he was innocent.

19 **trivial** [tríviəl]

adj. of little importance or value (syn) minor (ant) major

trivial problem

→ Sue has a **trivial** problem she needs to solve.

20 **unite** [jú:nait]

v. to bring together as one (ant) separate

unite ~ into

→ He **united** the individual states into one country.

Unit 18 Exercise

A Match the words with their definitions.

1. congress	•	•	a. a negative feeling based on emotion rather than fact
2. reverse	•	•	b. to create or start
3. political	•	•	c. a large meeting held to discuss ideas or policies
4. establish	•	•	d. to persuade a person to one's opinion
5. prejudice	•	•	e. opposite in method, direction, order, etc.
6. candidate	•	•	f. a person who is trying to win an office, job, award, etc.
7. convince	•	•	g. the coming together of people for a purpose
8. assembly	•	•	h. relating to the act of ruling or governing

B Circle the two words in each group that are opposites.

1. a. allow	b. convince	c. prejudice	d. forbid
2. a. reverse	b. trivial	c. political	d. major
3. a. least	b. aid	c. principal	d. democracy
4. a. state	b. positive	c. negative	d. unite

C Circle the words that best fit the sentences.

1. We will govern | aid those people in need.

2. Brian stated | established , "I'm really hungry now."

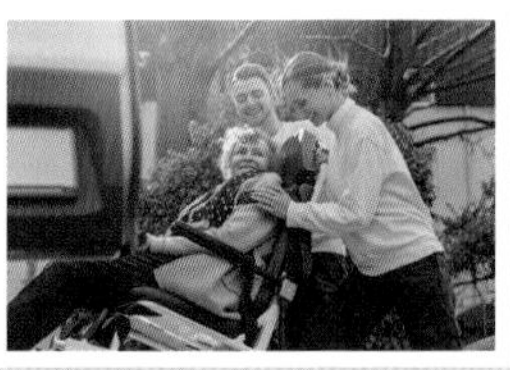

3. You need a congress | license to open a store in this city.

4. They hope the two countries will forbid | unite in the future.

5. There are too many trivial | corrupt people in business today.

6. People are demonstrating | stating against the government in the park.

D Choose the correct words to complete the sentences.

1. In a _______________, people have the right to vote.

a. democracy b. license c. assembly d. congress

2. The mayor of the city _______________ it very poorly.

a. govern b. forbids c. establishes d. convinces

3. This seems _______________, but it is important to me.

a. reverse b. corrupt c. trivial d. principal

4. Noah does not belong to a _______________ party.

a. reverse b. political c. negative d. democracy

5. The students will _______________ a new club at their school.

a. establish b. unite c. convince d. demonstrate

E Read the passage. Then, fill in the blanks.

Many countries around the world have **political** systems that are **democracies**. So there are elections for different positions in the government. **Candidates** for these positions **state** their beliefs. They try to **convince** people to vote for them. Then, when there is an election, voters support their favorite **candidates**. The winners get to **establish** a government and **govern** the country.

Some people may dislike the way that the **political** leaders are **governing**. They have **negative** views of the government. These people often think politicians are **corrupt** and do not **aid** regular citizens. They frequently **demonstrate** against these **corrupt** politicians. They try to **unite** the people in their country to support them in their views. Then, when there is another election, they hope voters elect different **candidates**.

1. In _______________, there are elections for positions in the government.

2. The candidates that win elections _______________ the country.

3. Some people have _______________ views of the government.

4. When there are _______________ politicians, some people demonstrate.

Unit 19 Word List

1 **capacity** [kəpǽsəti]
n. the ability to receive or hold
small capacity
→ Some buses have a small **capacity**.

2 **coal** [koul]
n. a dark mineral that can be burned and used for fuel
burn coal
→ The power company burns **coal** to make electricity.

3 **creep** [kri:p]
v. to move very slowly
creep on the highway
→ Cars are **creeping** on the highway because of the traffic jam.

4 **current** [kə́:rənt]
adv. currently
adj. belonging to the present time (syn) recent
current problem
→ One **current** problem is the lack of jobs.

5 **emission** [imíʃən]
n. something that is sent out (syn) discharge
harmful emission
→ Many vehicles release harmful **emissions**.

6 **fade** [feid]
v. to lose brightness or to become dim (ant) brighten
fade away
→ Sunlight is quickly **fading** away as the day ends.

7 **fasten** [fǽsən]
v. to fix one thing to another (ant) release
fasten one's seatbelt
→ Please **fasten** your seatbelt before takeoff.

8 **immediate** [imí:diət]
adv. immediately
adj. happening at once and without delay
immediate response
→ Jake got an **immediate** response to his question.

9 **innovation** [ìnəvéiʃən]
n. something that is new or recently introduced
innovation in
→ There are many **innovations** in technology nowadays.

10 **lodge** [lɑdʒ]
n. a small house where people may stay for a short time (syn) cabin
v. to stay at a hotel or inn
hunting lodge → Doug owns a hunting **lodge** in the countryside.
lodge at → We plan to **lodge** at a five-star hotel.

Unit 19

11 **maintain** [meintéin]

v. to keep in good condition or order (syn) preserve

maintain a car

→ He **maintains** the cars for use by the workers.

12 **mass** [mæs]

adj. massive

adj. relating to a large number of people

n. many things grouped together

mass transit → **Mass** transit like subways is common in big cities.

large mass → There is a large **mass** of people in the park.

13 **outstanding** [àutstǽndiŋ]

adj. excellent (syn) superb (ant) terrible

outstanding performance

→ The singer gave an **outstanding** performance.

14 **pace** [peis]

n. a rate of movement

fast pace

→ Traffic is moving at a fast **pace** today.

15 **roam** [roum]

v. to move from place to place, often with no purpose

roam around

→ We will **roam** around the city when we get there.

16 **sail** [seil]

n. sailor

v. to travel over water

n. a large cloth that catches the wind and moves a ship

sail away → The ship **sailed** away from the island.

raise a sail → Let's raise the **sail** and go.

17 **soar** [sɔːr]

v. to fly at a great height

soar high in the sky

→ The airplane **soared** high in the sky.

18 **vessel** [vésəl]

n. any craft that can travel on water (syn) ship, boat

sailing vessel

→ That sailing **vessel** can carry many people.

19 **voyage** [vɔ́iidʒ]

n. a long trip (syn) journey

go on a voyage

→ We are going on a **voyage** to South America.

20 **wreck** [rek]

n. the destruction of a ship, car, truck, etc.

v. to cause an accident involving a ship, car, truck

be in a wreck → Four vehicles were in the **wreck**.

wreck a car → Ellen **wrecked** her car by being careless.

Unit 19 Exercise

A Circle the words that fit the definitions.

1. happening at once and without delay

   a. mass b. immediate c. current d. outstanding

2. to move very slowly

   a. fasten b. creep c. sail d. lodge

3. to fly at a great height

   a. wreck b. roam c. fade d. soar

4. many things grouped together

   a. mass b. innovation c. capacity d. voyage

5. a dark mineral that can be burned and used for fuel

   a. capacity b. sail c. coal d. wreck

B Choose and write the correct words for the blanks.

fasten	vessel	maintain	fade	outstanding	emission

1. brighten ≠ ______________
2. discharge = ______________
3. terrible ≠ ______________
4. release ≠ ______________
5. preserve = ______________
6. ship = ______________

C Circle the words that best fit the sentences.

1. John ran the race at a slow pace | voyage .
2. There are many sick people during mass | current times.
3. She fastened | lodged at a resort during her vacation.

4. There was a major vessel | wreck on the highway this morning.
5. Thomas Edison's innovations | paces helped people around the world.
6. The warehouse has the capacity | innovation to hold large amounts of goods.

D Choose the correct words to complete the sentences.

1. The animals are ______________ around the grasslands.

a. wrecking b. roaming c. maintaining d. lodging

2. The ______________ to the middle of the rainforest took weeks.

a. capacity b. emission c. voyage d. vessel

3. We will ______________ our ship around the world.

a. soar b. sail c. fasten d. pace

4. The colors on the painting are starting to ______________.

a. fasten b. lodge c. wreck d. fade

5. The cat is ______________ up on the mouse from behind.

a. maintaining b. creeping c. soaring d. massing

E Read the passage. Then, write T for true or F for false.

Eric does not have a job at the **current** time. So he decides to travel around the world. It will be a long **voyage**, but he does not mind. He finds a **vessel** and gets ready to **sail**. He fills his ship to **capacity** with food and water. He does not need any **coal** because he plans to use the **sail** instead.

At first, Eric sets a fast **pace**. His ship does not have much **mass**, so it **sails** across the ocean quickly. Eric works hard to **maintain** his ship. He has **outstanding** repair skills, so he fixes everything that breaks. After a while, Eric decides to take his time. He **roams** across the ocean and travels from island to island. Two years later, he returns home.

1. Eric wants to travel only to one country. ________

2. Eric's ship is a vessel that can sail. ________

3. Eric's ship sails across the ocean slowly. ________

4. Eric roams across the ocean for two years. ________

Unit 20 Word List

1 **absolutely** [ǽbsəlù:tli]
adv. completely (syn) totally
absolutely right
→ You are **absolutely** right about that.

2 **alternative** [ɔ:ltə́:rnətiv]
adj. referring to a possible different solution, method, etc.
alternative energy
→ **Alternative** energy such as solar power is popular.

3 **angle** [ǽŋgl]
n. the space between two lines that meet at the same point
right angle
→ A right **angle** is ninety degrees.

4 **compound** [kámpaund]
adj. having two or more parts, ingredients, etc. (syn) complex
n. any combination of two or more parts
compound sentence → A **compound** sentence has two parts.
chemical compound → The chemical **compound** is made of three elements.

5 **contain** [kəntéin]
n. container
v. to hold or include in an area
contain water
→ The swimming pool **contains** water.

6 **device** [diváis]
n. a thing made for a certain purpose (syn) machine
electronic device
→ A computer is an electronic **device**.

7 **dimension** [diménʃən], [daiménʃən]
n. a measurement of length, width, or depth
three dimensions
→ A cube exists in three **dimensions**.

8 **extraordinary** [ikstrɔ́:rdənèri]
adj. past what is usual or normal (syn) amazing
extraordinary performance
→ Robert gave an **extraordinary** performance last night.

9 **flame** [fleim]
n. a burning gas coming from something like wood or coal (syn) fire
bright flame
→ This produces a bright **flame** when it burns.

10 **microscope** [máikrəskòup]
adj. microscopic
n. a tool that can let people see small objects more clearly
electron microscope
→ An electron **microscope** can see tiny things.

Unit 20

11 **mineral**
[mínərəl]

n. a type of rock often obtained from mining
valuable mineral
→ Gold and silver are valuable **minerals**.

12 **physics**
[fíziks]
adj. physicist

n. the science of matter, energy, motion, and force
nuclear physics
→ Emily will study nuclear **physics** in college.

13 **pollutant**
[pəlú:tənt]

n. something that makes the air, soil, or water unclean
harmful pollutant
→ Cars release harmful **pollutants** into the air.

14 **proof**
[pru:f]

n. evidence that something is true
provide proof
→ You must provide **proof** that you are correct.

15 **reveal**
[riví:l]

v. to make known or exhibit something (syn) show, display
reveal the answer
→ I will **reveal** the answer to you now.

16 **seek**
[si:k]
seek - sought - sought

v. to look for in order to obtain (syn) search
seek a solution
→ Tom is **seeking** a solution to the problem.

17 **series**
[sí(:)əri:z]

n. a group of similar or related things, events, etc.
read a series
→ Ken is reading a **series** of books by his favorite author.

18 **signal**
[sígnəl]

n. something that warns, guides, or directs others (syn) sign
v. to communicate a movement or sound to others
turn signal → Wait for the turn **signal** before you cross the street.
signal somebody → We will **signal** others so that they are careful.

19 **synthetic**
[sinθétik]

adj. relating to something made in a chemical process (ant) natural
synthetic material
→ The shirt is made of a **synthetic** material.

20 **wither**
[wíðər]

v. to dry up due to a lack of moisture (ant) grow
wither away
→ The flowers **withered** away in the hot sun.

Unit 20 Exercise

A Circle the correct definitions for the given words.

1. absolutely

a. a measurement of length, width, or depth
b. completely
c. the science of matter, energy, motion, and force
d. past what is usual or normal

2. series

a. a type of rock often obtained from mining
b. evidence that something is true
c. a group of similar or related things, events, etc.
d. a thing made for a certain purpose

3. seek

a. to hold or include in an area
b. to dry up due to a lack of moisture
c. to look for in order to obtain
d. to make known or exhibit something

4. flame

a. something that warns, guides, or directs others
b. a burning gas coming from something like wood or coal
c. a tool that can let people see small objects more clearly
d. the space between two lines that meet at the same point

B Circle the two words in each group that have the same meaning.

1. a. angle	b. pollutant	c. complex	d. compound
2. a. signal	b. sign	c. mineral	d. dimension
3. a. reveal	b. contain	c. display	d. seek
4. a. flame	b. machine	c. synthetic	d. device

C Circle the words that best fit the sentences.

1. John wants to major in angle | physics at college.

2. The grass contained | withered and died without any water.

3. These pollutants | alternatives are harming the ground and water.

4. Emily wrote an extraordinary | alternative paper and got an A+.

5. The scientist uses a mineral | microscope to look at small objects.

6. Something with two physics | dimensions has length and width.

D Choose the correct words to complete the sentences.

1. We took an ______________ road since the main one was busy.
   a. synthetic b. alternative c. compound d. extraordinary

2. There are many valuable ______________ buried in the ground here.
   a. microscopes b. signals c. minerals d. flames

3. He has no ______________ that he bought the item.
   a. dimension b. angle c. pollutant d. proof

4. That jar ______________ some tea she just made.
   a. reveals b. seeks c. withers d. contains

5. Plastic is a ______________ material made in factories.
   a. synthetic b. physics c. alternative d. device

E Read the passage. Then, fill in the blanks.

These days, science is more advanced than it used to be. Scientists are making **extraordinary** discoveries every day. Thanks to modern technology, they use **devices** such as **microscopes**. These tools can **reveal** information that provides **proof** of their theories.

Some scientists are developing **alternative** sources of energy. They are worried about the **pollutants** in the air. They believe humans **absolutely** must use different types of energy. They **seek** to create **synthetic** fuels. These fuels are special chemical **compounds**. They do not send **pollutants** into the air. Instead, they let people use machines without making the Earth dirty. Other scientists are doing research on various **minerals**. They think they can create new metals that are strong but light. When they are successful, they will **reveal** their creations to the world.

1. Scientists make extraordinary discoveries by using ______________ like microscopes.
2. Some scientists make ______________ energy sources.
3. Scientists want to make synthetic fuels that do not create ______________.
4. Successful scientists will ______________ the creations they make in the future.

Review 04 Units 16~20

A Choose and write the correct words for the definitions.

series	convince	laughter	priest
trivial	exaggerate	proof	fade

1. a person who performs religious duties ➡ ____________
2. a group of similar or related things, events, etc. ➡ ____________
3. to say that something is greater than reality ➡ ____________
4. to lose brightness or become dim ➡ ____________
5. to persuade a person to one's opinion ➡ ____________
6. a sound that shows amusement ➡ ____________
7. evidence that something is true ➡ ____________
8. of little importance or value ➡ ____________

B Circle the words that are the most similar to the underlined words.

1. Fred will take his <u>ship</u> all the way across the sea.
   a. wreck   b. coal   c. vessel   d. lodge

2. It is <u>wrong</u> to take something without paying for it.
   a. illegal   b. obvious   c. voluntary   d. deliberate

3. They will <u>search</u> for an answer until they find one.
   a. contain   b. seek   c. wither   d. signal

4. It was a <u>tragedy</u> when the hurricane destroyed the town.
   a. decade   b. patent   c. meteor   d. disaster

5. Tina <u>founded</u> the math club at her school last year.
   a. established   b. demonstrated   c. reversed   d. governed

C Choose the correct forms of the words to complete the sentences.

1. Jim suffered a severe | severely injury in a car accident.
2. Eric studies physicist | physics and knows a lot about it.
3. During current | currently times, many people have jobs.
4. She often uses her charm | charming to get what she wants.
5. The country is a democratic | democracy, so there are elections.

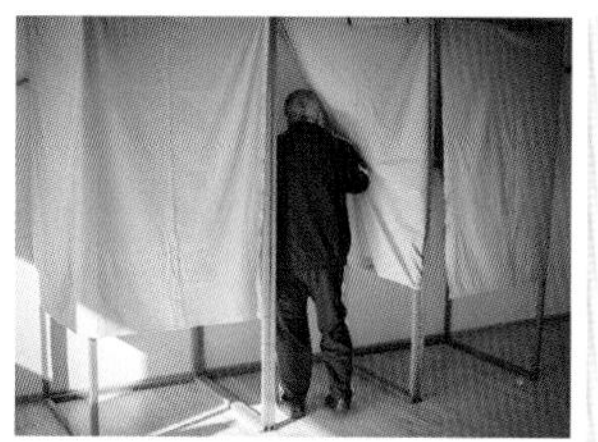

D Complete the sentences with the words in the box.

1. We have ______________ feelings about watching that movie.
2. The plants will ______________ if they get no water.
3. Someone is ______________ around in the forest.
4. There was an ______________ at the volcano this morning.
5. Let me ______________ that question and come up with an answer.

wither
creeping
negative
eruption
ponder

E Write the correct phrases in the blanks.

building a canal	feels envy	driver's license
extraordinary performance	fasten your seatbelt	urban environments

1. Please ______________________ before we start to drive.
2. Peter got his ______________________ when he was nineteen.
3. She ______________________ when her friends do something well.
4. ______________________ can be dangerous places at night.
4. They are ______________________ to connect the river to the sea.
5. They watched an ______________________ at the theater.

F Circle the mistakes. Then, write the correct sentences.

1. This box container some old clothes.

   ➡ ______________________________

2. The president is in the middle of a politics crisis.

   ➡ ______________________________

3. He achieved famous for winning a gold medal.

   ➡ ______________________________

4. I made an immediately reply to the email.

   ➡ ______________________________

5. It is rude to interruption people having a conversation.

   ➡ ______________________________

G Complete the crossword puzzle.

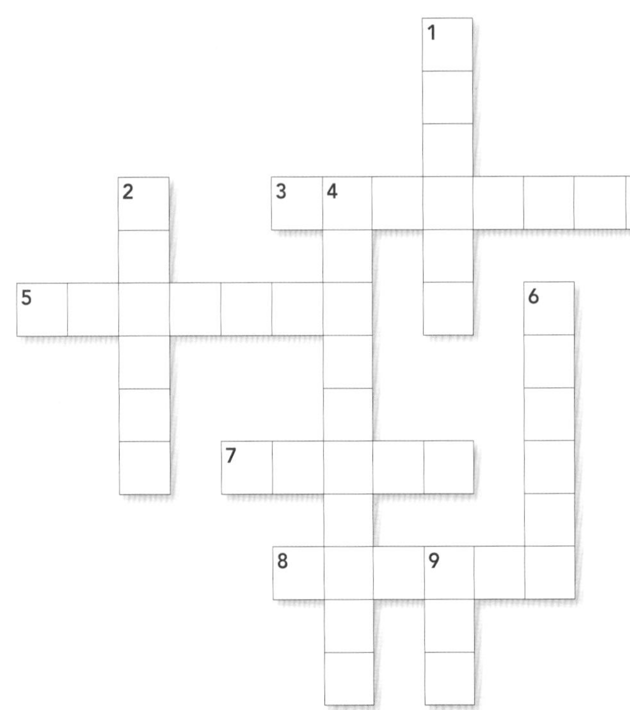

Across

3. the ability to receive or hold
5. easily seen or understood
7. to make a short stop
8. a period lasting ten years

Down

1. a long trip
2. to rule over others
4. completely
6. a thing made for a certain purpose
9. to provide support or help

H Read the passage. Then, answer the questions below.

Ancient Times

The fields of history and **archaeology** have **revealed** very much about ancient **civilizations**. For **instance**, many historians used to think that ancient people were not advanced. But that is **absolutely** wrong. Instead, people in ancient times made some **extraordinary innovations**. And some cultures were quite advanced.

Today, people **acknowledge** that some cultures had **outstanding** sailing **vessels**. They went on long **voyages** as they **roamed** the oceans. The Mesopotamians created an **urban** culture and built lots of **canals**. The ancient Greeks **established** a great society. Their **political** system was **democracy**. They **united** their people and **guaranteed** rights to citizens. Their scientists created various **devices** in an effort to **seek** knowledge. In ancient Rome, **honor** was very important. The Romans also created an empire that was the **envy** of people everywhere.

1. What is the passage mainly about?

a. the ancient Greeks

b. advanced ancient civilizations

c. the Romans and Mesopotamians

d. the fields of history and archaeology

2. What did the Mesopotamians have?

a. sailing vessels
b. scientific devices
c. a political system
d. lots of canals

3. What was important in ancient Rome?

a. envy
b. laughter
c. honor
d. democracy

4. What did many historians use to think?

➡ ______________________________

5. What did ancient Greek scientists do?

➡ ______________________________

Unit 21 Word List

1 **abstract** [ǽbstrækt]

adj. relating to something that is not specific

abstract art

→ Monet was a famous painter of **abstract** art.

2 **alter** [ɔ́:ltər]

v. to change (syn) modify

completely alter

→ Kevin completely **altered** the drawing by coloring parts of it.

3 **carve** [kɑ:rv]

v. to form something by cutting it (syn) slice

carve a statue

→ Erika will **carve** a statue from that piece of wood.

4 **clay** [klei]

n. an earthy material that is often used to make pots

make with clay

→ The students will make vases with **clay**.

5 **complicated** [kámpləkèitid]
n. complication

adj. composed of various parts that are connected (ant) simple

complicated plan

→ Nobody could understand the **complicated** plan.

6 **curve** [kə:rv]

n. a line that bends without angles

v. to bend in a circular motion

make a curve → The path makes a **curve** beside the lake.

curve sharply → The road **curves** sharply soon.

7 **dozen** [dʌ́zən]

n. a group of twelve

a dozen eggs

→ Jeff bought a **dozen** eggs at the store.

8 **engrave** [ingréiv]

v. to put letters, numbers, etc. on a hard surface

engrave one's name

→ He **engraved** his wife's name on the wedding ring.

9 **essence** [ésəns]
adj. essential

n. the basic nature or feature of a thing

essence of

→ What is the **essence** of this work of art?

10 **evident** [évidənt]
n. evidence

adj. clear to see or understand (syn) obvious (ant) unclear

evident that

→ It is **evident** that Lucy is an excellent painter.

11 **frame** [freim]

n. a case that a picture is put into
picture frame
→ She bought a picture **frame** to hang on her wall.

12 **knot** [nɑt]

n. a piece of rope drawn tight to fasten something
tie a knot
→ You must tie a **knot** on your shoe after putting it on.

13 **legend** [lédʒənd]
adj. legendary

n. a story handed down by tradition (syn) myth
Greek legend
→ Heracles was a great hero in Greek **legend**.

14 **literacy** [lítərəsi]

n. the ability to read and write
literacy rate
→ The **literacy** rate in many countries is almost 100%.

15 **media** [mí:diə]

n. means of communication such as newspapers, TV, etc.
mass media
→ Most people get their news from the mass **media**.

16 **pottery** [pátəri]

n. pots and vases that are made from clay
make pottery
→ We learned to make **pottery** in art class.

17 **remarkable** [rimá:rkəbl]

adj. impressive or extraordinary (syn) amazing
remarkable idea
→ Jeff told everyone about his **remarkable** idea.

18 **sheet** [ʃi:t]

n. a thin piece of cloth used to sleep on; a piece of paper
wash a sheet → You should wash the **sheets** after using them.
sheet of paper → Write the essay on a **sheet** of paper.

19 **string** [striŋ]

n. a thin or thick cord or thread
tie a string
→ Tie the **string** tightly so that it does not get loose.

20 **tale** [teil]

n. a story that describes a real or imaginary event
tell a tale
→ They told some **tales** at night around the campfire.

Unit 21 Exercise

A Match the words with their definitions.

1. curve •	• a. a piece of rope drawn tight to fasten something
2. literacy •	• b. a thin piece of cloth used to sleep on
3. clay •	• c. the ability to read and write
4. knot •	• d. a case that a picture is put into
5. frame •	• e. a thin or thick cord or thread
6. engrave •	• f. to put letters, numbers, etc. on a hard surface
7. sheet •	• g. an earthy material that is often used to make pots
8. string •	• h. to bend in a circular motion

B Write S for synonym or A for antonym next to each pair of words.

1. ________ unclear – evident
2. ________ amazing – remarkable
3. ________ carve – slice
4. ________ complicated – simple
5. ________ modify – alter
6. ________ legend – myth

C Circle the words that best fit the sentences.

1. He has an abstract | string painting style.
2. Let me tell you a knot | tale from long ago.
3. I need a clay | dozen boxes to put my things in.

4. Can you explain the essence | sheet of the idea?
5. Many people do not trust the sheet | media these days.
6. He bumped into the pottery | curve and knocked it down.

D Choose the correct words to complete the sentences.

1. We will ______________ the team's name on the trophy.

a. engrave b. curve c. knot d. string

2. Few people like to remember ______________ instructions.

a. alter b. string c. complicated d. pottery

3. It took the artist a while to ______________ a figure from the block.

a. engrave b. knot c. carve d. curve

4. I enjoy reading ______________ from ancient times.

a. dozens b. essences c. pottery d. legends

5. The path ______________ sharply when it gets near the stream.

a. engraves b. alters c. carves d. curves

E Read the passage. Then, write T for true or F for false.

At school one day, the students learn about art. The teacher says that there are many kinds of art. First, she shows the students some pictures in **frames**. Some of the pictures look realistic, but others look **abstract**. Some of the pictures are **complicated** while others are simple.

Then, the teacher mentions that **pottery** can also be art. She shows the students how to make **pottery** with **clay**. The students think that is **remarkable**. Next, the teacher tells the students some **tales** and **legends** about art in the past. It is **evident** to the students that art is very important, so they concentrate on the teacher's words. They really enjoy the class. When the class finishes, the students are sad that they cannot learn any more.

1. The teacher shows the students pictures in frames. ________

2. The teacher says that pottery is not art. ________

3. The students hear some tales about art. ________

4. It is evident to the students that art is not important. ________

Unit 22 Word List

1 **adequate** [ǽdəkwit]

adj. as good or as much as necessary

adequate amount

→ Kate ran for an **adequate** amount of time.

2 **barrier** [bǽriər]

n. anything that prevents passage or entry (syn) obstacle

stone barrier

→ A stone **barrier** was set up across the road.

3 **bunch** [bʌntʃ]

n. a collection or group of things

bunch of grapes

→ I ate a **bunch** of grapes for a snack.

4 **consequence** [kánsəkwèns]

n. the result of something that already happened (ant) cause

good consequence

→ We expect good **consequences** from our choice.

5 **consist** [kənsíst]

v. to be made up of (syn) comprise

consist of

→ The contest **consists** of running and swimming activities.

6 **crucial** [krúːʃəl]

adj. important (syn) vital (ant) unimportant

crucial time

→ The next few days are a **crucial** time for Mr. Smith.

7 **duplicate** *n.* [djúːpləkit] *v.* [djúplikeit]

n. a copy that looks like the original

v. to make an exact copy of

make a duplicate → Please make a **duplicate** of this report.

duplicate an image → He **duplicated** the images with a printer.

8 **efficiency** [ifíʃənsi] *adj.* efficient

n. the ability to do something without wasting time, money, etc.

improve one's efficiency

→ You must improve your **efficiency** when you exercise.

9 **firm** [fəːrm]

adj. solid or hard

firm ground

→ People should only run on **firm** ground.

10 **instant** [ínstənt]

n. a short period of time

adj. immediate (syn) prompt

in an instant → Someone will open the door in an **instant**.

instant results → Her hard work produced **instant** results.

11 **minimal** [mínəməl]

adj. the least possible or very small (syn) slight

minimal cost

→ James joined the gym at a **minimal** cost to himself.

12 **nerve** [nəːrv]

adj. nervous

n. a part of the body that produces various sensations; courage

every nerve → Every **nerve** in Rachel's body was tense.

build up one's nerve → It can take time to build up your **nerves**.

13 **outcome** [áutkʌ̀m]

n. the result of an action or activity

positive outcome

→ She is hoping for a positive **outcome** this weekend.

14 **pressure** [préʃər]

n. the use of a force on another body

v. to try to make someone do something

air pressure → The air **pressure** is dropping quickly.

pressure someone → Dave **pressured** Tim into working late at night.

15 **reluctant** [rilʌ́ktənt]

adj. unwilling to do something (ant) eager

reluctant to

→ Anna is **reluctant** to run in the race next week.

16 **several** [sévərəl]

adj. being more than two but not many

several ideas

→ We came up with **several** ideas.

17 **steep** [stiːp]

adj. going up at a high angle (syn) sharp

steep hill

→ It is hard to cycle up the **steep** hill.

18 **strict** [strikt]

strict - stricter - strictest

adj. demanding that rules, etc. should be followed (syn) severe

strict teacher

→ Ms. Richardson is a very **strict** teacher.

19 **substitute** [sʌ́bstitjùːt]

n. a person acting instead of another

substitute teacher

→ We had a **substitute** teacher during science class.

20 **vary** [vɛ́(ː)əri]

adj. various

v. to change in form, appearance, number, etc. (syn) differ

vary in

→ These snacks all **vary** in price and taste.

Unit 22 Exercise

A Circle the words that fit the definitions.

1. the ability to do something without wasting time, money, etc.
   a. bunch b. efficiency c. substitute d. outcome
2. demanding that rules, etc. should be followed
   a. instant b. strict c. firm d. several
3. a part of the body that produces various sensations
   a. consequence b. pressure c. nerve d. substitute
4. anything that prevents passage or entry
   a. outcome b. efficiency c. instant d. barrier
5. to try to make someone do something
   a. consist b. pressure c. vary d. duplicate

B Choose and write the correct words for the blanks.

consist	minimal	reluctant	vary	consequence	crucial

1. cause ≠ ____________ 2. eager ≠ ____________
3. comprise = ____________ 4. slight = ____________
5. unimportant ≠ ____________ 6. differ = ____________

C Circle the words that best fit the sentences.

1. Bake the cake until the center is instant | firm .
2. You can use honey as a nerve | substitute for butter.

3. Faith only did an instant | adequate amount of work.
4. There are several | steep people who want to talk to you.
5. A bunch | pressure of new workers showed up this morning.
6. Nobody is sure about the outcome | substitute of the game.

D Choose the correct words to complete the sentences.

1. The machine was able to ______________ the items easily.
   a. pressure b. consist c. duplicate d. efficiency

2. Melissa drinks ______________ coffee since she lacks time to make it.
   a. several b. instant c. minimal d. firm

3. Parts of this mountain are too ______________ to climb.
   a. steep b. adequate c. crucial d. strict

4. His duties ______________ of meeting customers and selling them products.
   a. duplicate b. vary c. consist d. pressure

5. It is ______________ that you follow these directions.
   a. reluctant b. crucial c. firm d. minimal

E Read the passage. Then, fill in the blanks.

People are very busy these days. Most of them work or study. They feel lots of **pressure** because of their jobs or school. Then, they go home. They are **reluctant** to do anything else because they are tired. However, it is **crucial** that they exercise. Even doing a **minimal** amount of exercise can help someone.

If people do not exercise, there could be **several** bad **consequences**. So doing exercise is important. It is also easy. People can exercise an **adequate** amount by doing a few hours a week. They can do a **bunch** of different activities, including jogging, playing a sport, and swimming. If they **vary** the exercises they do, they will have fun. And the **outcome** will be positive. They will get **instant** results, and they will feel great.

1. People feel ______________ because of their work or school.

2. It is crucial to do a ______________ amount of exercise.

3. There are a ______________ of different exercises people can do.

4. The ______________ of doing exercise will be positive for people.

Unit 23 Word List

1	**abandon** [əbǽndən]	*v.* to leave or give up (syn) quit abandon ship → Everyone **abandoned** ship when it started to sink.
2	**clue** [klu:]	*n.* anything that helps solve a problem (syn) hint find a clue → The police found a **clue** and solved the case.
3	**deny** [dinái]	*v.* to state that something is not true (syn) reject (ant) agree deny a fact → He lied and **denied** a fact.
4	**depress** [diprés] *adj.* depressed	*v.* to make very sad or unhappy depress someone → The difficult test **depressed** the students.
5	**despair** [dispέər]	*n.* the loss of hope feel despair → Elaine felt **despair** when she lost her job.
6	**employ** [implɔ́i] *n.* employer	*v.* to give a person a job (syn) hire (ant) fire employ at → Harry is **employed** at a large company.
7	**enable** [inéibl]	*v.* to make something possible or easy (syn) allow enable to → Fred **enabled** me to learn math.
8	**frighten** [fráitən] *adj.* frightened	*v.* to scare (syn) terrify frighten very much → The strange sound **frightened** us very much.
9	**indicate** [índəkèit]	*v.* to show or point out indicate that → The sign **indicates** that the park is close to us.
10	**insist** [insíst]	*v.* to be firm or to ask for something strongly (syn) demand insist that → Paul **insists** that we go to his house for dinner.

11 **justify** [dʒʌ́stəfài]

v. to show that something is right

justify one's opinion

→ Can you **justify** your opinion for us?

12 **lack** [læk]

v. not to have something needed or wanted

n. the state of not having enough of something

lack money → I can't go out because I **lack** money.

lack of → Nancy has a **lack** of time now.

13 **nasty** [nǽsti]

adj. unclean, ugly, or mean (ant) pleasant

nasty habit

→ Smoking is a very **nasty** habit.

14 **quarrel** [kwɔ́(:)rəl]

v. to fight (syn) argue

quarrel with

→ Anna **quarreled** with her parents about her grades.

15 **reward** [riwɔ́:rd]

n. money or something given for doing something (syn) prize

get a reward

→ Jake got a **reward** for finding the gold ring.

16 **scold** [skould]

v. to find fault with

scold someone

→ My mother **scolded** me for making a mess.

17 **sympathy** [símpəθi]

adj. sympathetic

n. a feeling of compassion or being sorry

feel sympathy

→ They felt **sympathy** toward the homeless man.

18 **threat** [θret]

v. threaten

n. a statement of one's intent to cause pain, punishment, etc.

serious threat

→ Edward received a serious **threat** from the gangster.

19 **urgent** [ə́:rdʒənt]

adj. requiring that something happen immediately

urgent matter

→ He has to solve an **urgent** matter now.

20 **weird** [wiərd]

adj. strange or unusual (ant) normal

weird noise

→ She heard a **weird** noise in the middle of the night.

Unit 23 Exercise

A Match the words with their definitions.

1. despair •	• a. to make very sad or unhappy
2. nasty •	• b. to show that something is right
3. insist •	• c. to be firm or to ask for something strongly
4. sympathy •	• d. the loss of hope
5. depress •	• e. anything that helps solve a problem
6. justify •	• f. unclean, ugly, or mean
7. clue •	• g. a statement of one's intent to cause pain, punishment, et
8. threat •	• h. a feeling of compassion or being sorry

B Circle the two words in each group that have the same meaning.

1. a. reject	b. deny	c. frighten	d. threat
2. a. insist	b. despair	c. quarrel	d. argue
3. a. reward	b. abandon	c. prize	d. justify
4. a. weird	b. allow	c. enable	d. sympathy

C Circle the words that best fit the sentences.

1. Some modern art looks very weird | urgent .
2. She lacks | scolds the ability to fix the problem.
3. The ghost denied | frightened everyone very much.
4. His company employs | indicates more than 500 people.
5. He received a(n) nasty | urgent phone call from the hospital.
6. I insisted | abandoned my dream of traveling around the world.

D **Choose the correct words to complete the sentences.**

1. I ______________ that I was ready to go home.
   a. lacked b. depressed c. indicated d. abandoned

2. The teacher ______________ the noisy students.
   a. scolded b. employed c. insisted d. quarreled

3. He received a ______________ for saving the man in the fire.
   a. despair b. clue c. reward d. sympathy

4. The computer ______________ people to work quickly nowadays.
   a. enables b. employs c. justifies d. scolds

5. He often ______________ about money with his friends.
   a. denies b. lacks c. abandons d. quarrels

E **Read the passage. Then, write T for true or F for false.**

David's company **employs** thousands of people. However, his job is **depressing** him lately. David has a new boss. And his boss is very **nasty**. His boss often **quarrels** with David and the other workers. He **scolds** them even when they do nothing wrong. He even makes **threats** sometimes.

David and his coworkers feel **despair**. They do not know what to do. They think their new boss is **weird** and **lacks sympathy** for others. They decide to complain to the company president. There is a big meeting. The boss cannot **justify** his bad behavior. He **insists** that he is doing a good job. But the president believes David and the others. He **scolds** the boss, tells him to go away, and gives a **reward** to the other employees.

1. David is the new boss at his company. ________
2. David's boss scolds the workers and makes threats. ________
3. David's boss does not have any sympathy for others. ________
4. The company president gives a reward to David's boss. ________

Unit 24 Word List

1 **attach** [ətǽtʃ]
n. attachment

v. to connect two things to each other (syn) fasten
attach ~ to
→ **Attach** the picture to the paper with glue.

2 **conform** [kənfɔ́ːrm]

v. to act according to the standards of a group (syn) obey
conform to
→ You must **conform** to the customs of this country.

3 **content**
adj. [kəntént]
n. [kɑ́ntent]

adj. satisfied with what one has
n. the topics covered in a book, article, etc.
content with → Marcia is **content** with her current situation.
good content → The book contains good **content** we can use.

4 **declare** [dikléər]

v. to say something out loud
declare that
→ George **declared** that he was quitting his job.

5 **despite** [dispáit]

prep. in spite of
despite the fact
→ **Despite** the fact that it was snowing, we went outside.

6 **dramatic** [drəmǽtik]

adj. sudden, surprising, or impressive
dramatic speech
→ The president gave a **dramatic** speech to the country.

7 **emphasize** [émfəsàiz]

v. to give great importance to (syn) stress
emphasize a point
→ Lucy **emphasized** her point during the meeting.

8 **faint** [feint]

v. to lose consciousness for a short time (syn) pass out
adj. lacking brightness or clearness (ant) bright
faint from → Sally **fainted** from a lack of food.
faint color → Dave uses **faint** colors when he paints.

9 **female** [fíːmèil]

n. a girl or woman (ant) male
adj. relating to a girl or woman
biological female → She is a biological **female**.
female role → Some cultures have **female** roles for women.

10 **generation** [dʒènəréiʃən]

n. everyone born and living around the same time
young generation
→ The young **generation** does not always listen well.

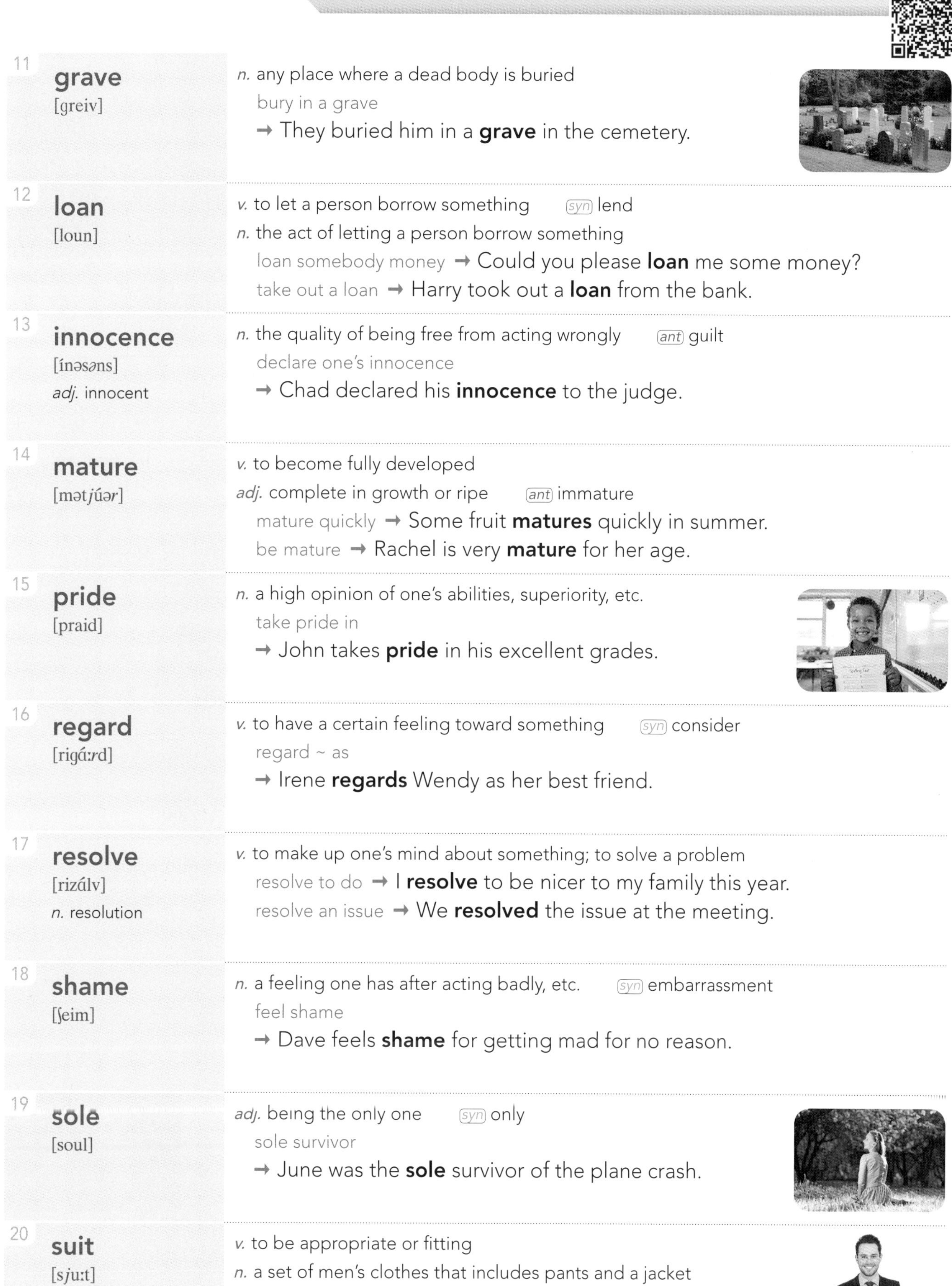

11 **grave**
[greiv]

n. any place where a dead body is buried
bury in a grave
→ They buried him in a **grave** in the cemetery.

12 **loan**
[loun]

v. to let a person borrow something (syn) lend
n. the act of letting a person borrow something
loan somebody money → Could you please **loan** me some money?
take out a loan → Harry took out a **loan** from the bank.

13 **innocence**
[ínəsəns]
adj. innocent

n. the quality of being free from acting wrongly (ant) guilt
declare one's innocence
→ Chad declared his **innocence** to the judge.

14 **mature**
[mətjúər]

v. to become fully developed
adj. complete in growth or ripe (ant) immature
mature quickly → Some fruit **matures** quickly in summer.
be mature → Rachel is very **mature** for her age.

15 **pride**
[praid]

n. a high opinion of one's abilities, superiority, etc.
take pride in
→ John takes **pride** in his excellent grades.

16 **regard**
[rigá:rd]

v. to have a certain feeling toward something (syn) consider
regard ~ as
→ Irene **regards** Wendy as her best friend.

17 **resolve**
[rizálv]
n. resolution

v. to make up one's mind about something; to solve a problem
resolve to do → I **resolve** to be nicer to my family this year.
resolve an issue → We **resolved** the issue at the meeting.

18 **shame**
[ʃeim]

n. a feeling one has after acting badly, etc. (syn) embarrassment
feel shame
→ Dave feels **shame** for getting mad for no reason.

19 **sole**
[soul]

adj. being the only one (syn) only
sole survivor
→ June was the **sole** survivor of the plane crash.

20 **suit**
[sju:t]
adj. suitable

v. to be appropriate or fitting
n. a set of men's clothes that includes pants and a jacket
suit someone → That dress really **suits** you.
wear a suit → Many men wear **suits** to their jobs.

Unit 24 Exercise

A Circle the words that fit the definitions.

1. sudden, surprising, or impressive

a. female b. mature c. faint d. dramatic

2. in spite of

a. mature b. despite c. sole d. suit

3. to have a certain feeling toward something

a. attach b. emphasize c. regard d. resolve

4. any place where a dead body is buried

a. grave b. pride c. loan d. innocence

5. the topics covered in a book, article, etc.

a. generation b. suit c. pride d. content

B Write S for synonym or A for antonym next to each pair of words.

1. ________ fasten – attach

2. ________ lend – loan

3. ________ bright – faint

4. ________ innocence – guilt

5. ________ female – male

6. ________ embarrassment – shame

C Circle the words that best fit the sentences.

1. Matt often wears a suit | shame to work.

2. She has a lot of female | pride in her job.

3. You can eat the fruit when it is sole | mature .

4. Do not conform | faint to other people's beliefs.

5. Every innocence | generation has its own style and culture.

6. The teacher emphasized | resolved the need to study hard.

D Choose the correct words to complete the sentences.

1. We ______________ to do our best on the project.
   a. resolved b. regarded c. suited d. matured

2. Jeremy ______________ that Tom was the winner.
   a. loaned b. conformed c. declared d. fainted

3. The ______________ contestant in the contest was Mr. Smith.
   a. sole b. mature c. content d. female

4. She felt ______________ for making her friend cry.
   a. loan b. shame c. generation d. suit

5. They put the body in a ______________ the other day.
   a. pride b. innocence c. grave d. generation

E Read the passage. Then, fill in the blanks.

In most families, two **generations** live together. Parents and their children are separate **generations**. In some places, three **generations**—children, parents, and grandparents—live in the same house. **Despite** the fact that the house may be crowded, this **suits** most families. Each person **conforms** to get along with the others. If there is a problem, the leader of the family **declares** a solution.

Nowadays, as young males and **females mature**, they often move out of their family home. They **regard** those living with others as crowded. They think living alone in a home is better. They may take out a **loan** to pay the rent for their home. They are often **content** by themselves. But many do not have enough money. So they **resolve** to move back home.

1. Sometimes three ______________ of a family live together.

2. Each person must ______________ to get along with everyone else.

3. When some people ______________, they decide to move out of their home.

4. Some people ______________ to return home if they cannot pay the rent.

Unit 25 Word List

1	**celebrity** [səlébrəti]	*n.* a famous or well-known person (syn) star become a celebrity → The actor became a **celebrity** last year.
2	**cite** [sait]	*v.* to mention in support or proof of (syn) quote cite a passage → Jeff **cited** a passage from the book in his report.
3	**corporate** [kɔ́ːrpərit] *n.* corporation	*adj.* relating to a business corporate matter → This is a **corporate** matter for the CEO to handle.
4	**critic** [krítik] *v.* criticize	*n.* a person who judges or evaluates movie critic → Most movie **critics** disliked the new film.
5	**curse** [kəːrs]	*n.* the expression of a desire that something bad happen *v.* to wish evil or bad luck on a person (ant) bless put a curse on → The fairy put a **curse** on Sleeping Beauty. curse somebody → The witch **cursed** the prince and gave him back luck.
6	**deal** [diːl] *n.* dealer	*v.* to take action on a person or thing *n.* a business act deal with → I do not have time to **deal** with any problems now. make a deal → Sal's company made a **deal** with WRT, Inc.
7	**effective** [iféktiv]	*adj.* acting properly and producing the expected result effective plan → Jasmine came up with an **effective** plan.
8	**engagement** [ingéidʒmənt]	*n.* an appointment or a plan to get married announce one's engagement → Lisa announced her **engagement** to Todd.
9	**fable** [féibl]	*n.* a short story, often with animals, that teaches a lesson Aesop's fables → *The Tortoise and the Hare* is one of Aesop's **fables**.
10	**foundation** [faundéiʃən]	*n.* the act of being created; the basis of something foundation of → The **foundation** of the business was in 2015. building foundation → The building **foundation** supports the whole structure.

11 **intervene**
[intərvíːn]

v. to come between two groups to help
intervene in
→ Terry **intervened** in the argument they were having.

12 **leather**
[léðər]

n. the skin of an animal that can be used for making things
leather shoes
→ He always wears **leather** shoes to work.

13 **memorable**
[mémərəbl]

adj. worth remembering (ant) forgettable
memorable day
→ We had a **memorable** day at the park.

14 **mostly**
[móustli]

adv. for the large part (syn) generally
mostly well
→ She is **mostly** well after her long illness.

15 **profit**
[prάfit]
adj. profitable

v. to make money (syn) earn
n. money that a person, company, store, etc. makes
profit a lot → Larry **profited** a lot from his invention.
make a profit → The store made a **profit** from selling computers.

16 **reform**
[rifɔ́ːrm]

v. to change to something better (syn) improve
n. a change that improves a situation (syn) improvement
reform the law → The president wants to **reform** the law.
need reform → This country needs **reform** in many fields.

17 **represent**
[rèprizént]

v. to stand, speak, or act for another person
represent one's country
→ The ambassador **represented** his country well.

18 **ruin**
[rúː(ː)in]

v. to damage something very much
n. the destroyed parts of a building
ruin a movie → He **ruined** the movie with his poor acting.
be in ruins → The whole city is in **ruins**.

19 **silence**
[sáiləns]

n. the absence of noise (syn) quiet (ant) loudness
in silence
→ I prefer to do my homework in **silence**.

20 **version**
[və́ːrʒən]

n. a particular form of something (syn) type
several versions
→ There are several **versions** of that song.

Unit 25 Exercise

A Match the words with their definitions.

1. corporate	•	•	a. money that a person, company, store, etc. makes
2. foundation	•	•	b. worth remembering
3. memorable	•	•	c. to wish evil or bad luck on a person
4. profit	•	•	d. relating to a business
5. critic	•	•	e. to come between two groups to help
6. curse	•	•	f. the act of being created; the basis of something
7. version	•	•	g. a particular form of something
8. intervene	•	•	h. a person who judges or evaluates

B Circle the two words in each group that have the same meaning.

1. a. curse	b. cite	c. effective	d. quote
2. a. reform	b. improve	c. profit	d. memorable
3. a. celebrity	b. intervene	c. quiet	d. silence
4. a. generally	b. effective	c. fable	d. mostly

C Circle the words that best fit the sentences.

1. Water got on the painting and cursed | ruined it.
2. At the end of the fable | profit is the moral of the story.
3. Thomas likes to wear a black leather | memorable jacket.
4. Everyone in the store recognized the celebrity | foundation .
5. The new plan was corporate | effective and worked perfectly.
6. Joanne told everyone about her engagement | version to Mark.

D Choose the correct words to complete the sentences.

1. Mr. Jenkins ______________ Peter during his court case.

a. intervened b. profited c. represented d. reformed

2. They made a ______________ to export products to Japan.

a. version b. deal c. fable d. curse

3. It is important to ______________ many of the schools.

a. cite b. profit c. intervene d. reform

4. The company will ______________ from its new items.

a. profit b. deal c. ruin d. represent

5. There was ______________ when the boss entered the room.

a. leather b. engagement c. silence d. foundation

E Read the passage. Then, write T for true or F for false.

Cindy decides to become a **celebrity**. She enjoys movies, so she wants to be an actor. She visits a film company. Cindy's agent **represents** her and makes a **deal**. She will star in a new movie. The film company and Cindy believe the movie **critics** will love it. They think it will make a **profit**, too.

Cindy and the other performers begin filming. They are making a modern **version** of an old film. They are sure it will be **memorable**. When the filming is **mostly** done, there is suddenly a problem. There is not enough money. Cindy is upset. She believes she suffers from a **curse**. Fortunately, someone **intervenes** and provides enough money to finish the film. It makes a **profit**, and Cindy becomes a famous **celebrity**.

1. Cindy's agent represents her to a movie company. ________

2. Cindy and the company think their movie will make a profit. ________

3. Cindy's friends think she is suffering from a curse. ________

4. Cindy does not become a famous celebrity. ________

Review 05 Units 21~25

A Choose and write the correct words for the definitions.

generation	pottery	insist	ruin
pressure	dramatic	clue	vary

1. to be firm or to ask for something strongly ➡ ______________
2. sudden, surprising, or impressive ➡ ______________
3. pots and vases that are made from clay ➡ ______________
4. the destroyed parts of a building ➡ ______________
5. to try to make someone do something ➡ ______________
6. anything that helps solve a problem ➡ ______________
7. to change in form, appearance, number, etc. ➡ ______________
8. everyone born and living around the same time ➡ ______________

B Circle the words that are the most similar to the underlined words.

1. The sight of the monster terrified everyone in the room.
   a. frightened b. scolded c. enabled d. depressed

2. Lisa believes the solution to the problem is obvious.
   a. complicated b. remarkable c. evident d. abstract

3. He quoted some sentences from another book in his report.
   a. represented b. cited c. intervened d. reformed

4. You need to make a slight change in your plans.
   a. firm b. adequate c. strict d. minimal

5. I will lend Thomas some books for a couple of weeks.
   a. loan b. attach c. emphasize d. resolve

C Choose the correct forms of the words to complete the sentences.

1. Your sad story really depression | depresses me.
2. Dogs and cats can maturity | mature very quickly.
3. We plan to profit | profitable by selling imported cars.
4. The lecture was too complication | complicated to understand.
5. She suffered some damage to her nerves | nervous while jogging.

D Complete the sentences with the words in the box.

foundation
pride
altered
strict
employed

1. Molly has a lot of ______________ in her long blond hair.
2. Everyone must follow the ______________ rules at the school.
3. The earthquake damaged the ______________ of the building.
4. Chris ______________ his brother at his company.
5. He ______________ the picture by painting over parts of it.

E Write the correct phrases in the blanks.

memorable day	adequate amount	wear a suit
get a reward	effective plan	sheets of paper

1. I do not usually ______________________ to work.
2. His ______________________ was a total success.
3. Sarah's birthday was such a ______________________.
4. He ate an ______________________ of food for dinner.
5. You will ______________________ for finding the missing cat.
6. She used five ______________________ to write her paper.

F Circle the mistakes. Then, write the correct sentences.

1. June will attachment the pictures to the email.

➡ ______________________________

2. He loves to read the legendary about Theseus and the Minotaur.

➡ ______________________________

3. The criticize wrote that she really enjoyed the play.

➡ ______________________________

4. The employees' efficient improved thanks to their training.

➡ ______________________________

5. There was a serious threaten on the life of the president.

➡ ______________________________

G Complete the crossword puzzle.

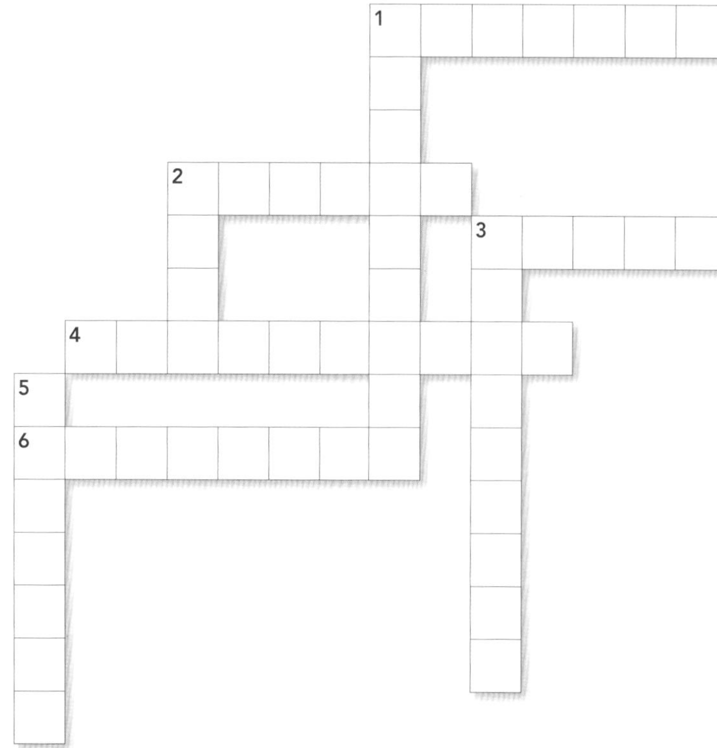

Across

1. to say something out loud
2. relating to a girl or woman
3. to form something by cutting it
4. impressive or extraordinary
6. to show or point out

Down

1. to make an exact copy of
2. solid or hard
3. a famous or well-known person
5. the absence of noise

H Read the passage. Then, answer the questions below.

David's School

The teachers at David's school insist that the students work hard. They **scold** and **frighten** lazy students and search for **effective** ways to teach everyone. There is also **pressure** on the students. They understand the **consequences** of low grades. If they do a **minimal** amount of work, they will do poorly. So they do not mind **strict** teachers.

In David's art class, he learns about **abstract** art and **pottery**. The teacher **emphasizes** the need to remember everything. She **declares** that some art looks **remarkable**, and she tells **several** interesting **tales** about the paintings. David does not normally like art, but he **resolves** to appreciate it. He writes a **memorable** essay for the class. David's teacher cites his essay in class, so he feels a great amount of **pride**.

1. What is the passage mainly about?

a. David's art class

b. reasons to study hard

c. the consequences of low grades

d. teachers and classes at David's school

2. What kind of teachers does David's school have?

a. efficient teachers b. kind teachers

c. boring teachers d. strict teachers

3. What does David's art teacher say about some art?

a. It looks remarkable. b. It is expensive.

c. It is cheap. d. It looks bad.

4. What do teachers do to lazy students?

➡ ______________________________

5. Why does David feel pride?

➡ ______________________________

Unit 26 Word List

1 **application** [æpləkéiʃən]

n. a request for a job, admission, etc.; the act of using something
job application → Paul filled out a job **application** at the store.
many applications → This invention has many **applications**.

2 **bid** [bid]

v. to offer to do work for a particular price
n. an order or offer (syn) proposal
bid on a contract → Mr. Smith hopes to **bid** on a contract.
make a bid → We will make a **bid** at the auction.

3 **boss** [bɑs]

n. a person who directs others (syn) manager
become a boss
→ Sara became a **boss** when she bought the company.

4 **central** [séntrəl]

adj. in or near the middle
central part
→ George lives in the **central** part of the city.

5 **contrary** [kɑ́ntreri]

adj. opposite in nature or direction (syn) different (ant) same
contrary opinion
→ Kevin has a **contrary** opinion about the matter.

6 **counsel** [káunsəl]
n. counselor

n. a piece of advice
v. to give advice, opinion, or instruction
provide counsel → I provided **counsel** when they asked for help.
counsel someone → Ms. Bryant **counseled** the boy on his problem.

7 **due** [dju:]

adj. owing or owed as a debt (syn) payable
be due
→ The electric bill is **due** tomorrow.

8 **enclose** [inklóuz]

v. to shut or surround on all sides
enclose a field
→ The farmer **enclosed** his fields with a fence.

9 **fulfill** [fulfíl]

v. to perform, satisfy, or carry out (syn) complete
fulfill one's duty
→ He **fulfilled** his duty during the day.

10 **fund** [fʌnd]

n. a supply of money for a certain purpose
retirement fund
→ She has a lot of money in her retirement **fund**.

11 **informal**
[infɔ́ːrməl]

adj. not according to an official way (syn) casual (ant) formal
informal clothes
→ Some workers are wearing **informal** clothes.

12 **index**
[índeks]

n. a listing of information and the page numbers it is found on in a book
in the index
→ You can find that information in the **index**.

13 **invest**
[invést]
n. investment

v. to use money in the hope of making more later
invest in
→ Many people **invest** in the stock market these days.

14 **network**
[nétwə̀ːrk]

n. a connected system of electric or communication devices
telephone network
→ The telephone **network** connects people around the world.

15 **region**
[ríːdʒən]
adj. regional

n. a large, continuous area of land (syn) place
local region
→ There are many factories in the local **region**.

16 **reservation**
[rèzərvéiʃən]

n. a booking to stay at or to use a hotel, airplane, etc.
hotel reservation
→ I have a hotel **reservation** for two nights.

17 **resign**
[rizáin]

v. to give up a job or other position (syn) quit
resign from
→ Paula **resigned** from her job and moved away.

18 **secretary**
[sékrətèri]

n. a person who does routine work in an office (syn) clerk
office secretary
→ Amy has a job as an office **secretary**.

19 **submit**
[səbmít]

v. to present something to others (syn) turn in
submit a report
→ He has to **submit** a report by Friday.

20 **vocation**
[voukéiʃən]

n. an occupation or business (syn) profession
as one's vocation
→ Stuart chose law as his **vocation**.

Unit 26 Exercise

A Circle the words that fit the definitions.

1. owing or owed as a debt
   a. informal　　b. due　　c. central　　d. contrary
2. a connected system of electric or communication devices
   a. fund　　b. reservation　　c. network　　d. index
3. a listing of information and the page numbers it is found on in a book
   a. region　　b. application　　c. vocation　　d. index
4. in or near the middle
   a. central　　b. informal　　c. contrary　　d. due
5. a supply of money for a certain purpose
   a. boss　　b. fund　　c. secretary　　d. bid

B Choose and write the correct words for the blanks.

vocation	secretary	contrary	bid	informal	fulfill

1. proposal = ________
2. formal ≠ ________
3. same ≠ ________
4. profession = ________
5. clerk = ________
6. complete = ________

C Circle the words that best fit the sentences.

1. This counsel | region of the country is mostly rural.
2. She will submit | invest her money by buying gold.
3. Alicia sent her network | application to the university.
4. They made a reservation | fund to eat at that restaurant.
5. I resigned | enclosed from my job because I was unhappy.
6. The boss | reservation held a meeting with all of the workers.

D Choose the correct words to complete the sentences.

1. They ______________ the city with a huge wall.
   a. invested b. resigned c. enclosed d. submitted

2. Please ______________ your homework by this Friday.
   a. submit b. counsel c. invest d. bid

3. She ______________ them to try their best.
   a. counseled b. resigned c. submitted d. fulfilled

4. They plan to make a ______________ on the apartment tomorrow.
   a. region b. vocation c. fund d. bid

5. Her new home ______________ all of her dreams.
   a. counseled b. submitted c. fulfilled d. invested

E Read the passage. Then, fill in the blanks.

At college, Scott decides on his **vocation**. He wants to **invest** money for people. So he studies economics. After he finishes school, he **submits applications** to many companies in the **region**. One company hires him, so he begins working there.

He develops a **network** of investors. He creates a **fund**, and it starts making money. One day, his **boss resigns**. He has an **informal** meeting with Scott. He **counsels** Scott to go with him to work at another company in the **central** part of the city. But Scott has a **contrary** idea. He refuses to **resign**. He decides to stay and **fulfill** his responsibilities to his investors. Scott becomes the new **boss** at his company. Everyone, including all of the **secretaries**, thinks he is the best **boss**.

1. Scott wants to ______________ money as his vocation.

2. Scott applies for jobs at some companies in the ______________.

3. Scott's boss ______________ him to work at another company.

4. Scott does not ______________ but continues working at his company.

Unit 27 Word List

1 **ash** [æʃ]

n. the powdery remains of something after it burns

burn ~ to ash

→ The forest fire burned the trees to **ash**.

2 **colony** [kάləni]

n. an area that is controlled by a powerful country

American colony

→ England lost its American **colonies** in the 1700s.

3 **define** [difáin]

n. definition

v. to say the meaning of

define a word

→ Please **define** this word for me.

4 **distinct** [distíŋkt]

n. distinction

adj. different in nature or quality (syn) separate (ant) similar

distinct feature

→ One **distinct** feature of the plant is its smell.

5 **fault** [fɔːlt]

n. the blame for a mistake or failure

one's fault

→ It is John's **fault** that the window broke.

6 **galaxy** [gǽləksi]

n. a large group of stars

Milky Way Galaxy

→ Earth is located in the Milky Way **Galaxy**.

7 **identity** [aidéntəti]

n. the condition or character of what a person or thing is

new identity

→ He needs a new **identity** to start his life over again.

8 **inherit** [inhérit]

v. to receive from one's ancestors

inherit money

→ She **inherited** some money from her grandparents.

9 **limb** [lim]

n. an arm or leg of an animal

artificial limb

→ Jeff lost his leg and needs an artificial **limb**.

10 **logical** [lάdʒikəl]

adj. making sense or expected (ant) illogical

logical thinking

→ Sherlock Holmes solves cases with **logical** thinking.

11 **overwhelming** [òuvərhwélmiŋ]

adj. so powerful that something is hard to resist

overwhelming victory

→ Our team won an **overwhelming** victory today.

12 **parallel** [pǽrəlèl]

adj. moving the same way but at the same distance and never meeting

parallel lines

→ Please draw two **parallel** lines on the paper.

13 **phenomenon** [finámənàn]
pl. phenomena

n. a fact or event that is observed

natural phenomenon

→ Lightning is a natural **phenomenon**.

14 **plain** [plein]

adj. clear and easily understood (ant) unclear

n. a flat area of land that has few or no trees

plain talk → Harry uses **plain** talk, so everyone understands him.

on the plain → Many cows are eating grass on the **plain**.

15 **roar** [rɔːr]

v. to make a loud, deep cry

roar loudly

→ The lion **roared** loudly and attacked.

16 **rust** [rʌst]

n. the red or orange coating that forms on iron (syn) decay

spot of rust

→ I can see a spot of **rust** on the car.

17 **shallow** [ʃǽlou]

adj. having little depth (ant) deep

shallow water

→ There is **shallow** water near the shore.

18 **sour** [sauər]

adj. having an acid taste like a lemon (ant) sweet

sour taste

→ Chris dislikes lemons because of their **sour** taste.

19 **sting** [stiŋ]
sting - stung - stung

v. to cause a sharp pain

sting suddenly

→ The bee **stung** the girl suddenly.

20 **tail** [teil]

n. the back part of an animal that forms a separate limb

wag one's tail

→ The friendly dog is wagging its **tail**.

Unit 27 Exercise

A Circle the correct definitions for the given words.

1. define
   a. to make a loud, deep cry
   b. to cause a sharp pain
   c. to receive from one's ancestors
   d. to say the meaning of

2. logical
   a. having little depth
   b. having an acid taste like a lemon
   c. making sense or expected
   d. so powerful that something is hard to resist

3. sting
   a. to cause a sharp pain
   b. to say the meaning of
   c. to receive from one's ancestors
   d. to make a loud, deep cry

4. phenomenon
   a. a large group of stars
   b. an arm or leg of an animal
   c. a fact or event that is observed
   d. the red or orange coating that forms on iron

B Circle the two words in each group that are opposites.

1. a. distinct	b. similar	c. galaxy	d. logical
2. a. parallel	b. rust	c. shallow	d. deep
3. a. unclear	b. define	c. colony	d. plain
4. a. sting	b. sweet	c. sour	d. phenomenon

C Circle the words that best fit the sentences.

1. The cat moved its rust | tail back and forth.
2. The train roared | inherited loudly as it went by.
3. He will inherit | sting a house from his parents.
4. There are billions of stars in that colony | galaxy .
5. Because of the volcano, a lot of ash | fault was in the air.
6. The army used logical | overwhelming force to win the battle.

D Choose the correct words to complete the sentences.

1. Whose ______________ is it that the door was unlocked?
   a. galaxy b. tail c. plain d. fault

2. The spy has a secret ______________ that nobody knows.
   a. phenomenon b. limb c. ash d. identity

3. There is too much ______________ on the playground equipment.
   a. colony b. rust c. tail d. galaxy

4. The two streets run ______________ to each other.
   a. parallel b. shallow c. sour d. distinct

5. He is suffering pain in one of his ______________.
   a. tails b. rusts c. identities d. limbs

E Read the passage. Then, write T for true or F for false.

There are billions of **galaxies** in the universe. The Earth is just one place in one **galaxy**. But it is a **distinct** place. There are all kinds of amazing life on the planet. There are **overwhelming** natural **phenomena** as well.

For example, there are large animals such as lions. When they **roar**, they can be very frightening. There are also tiny animals such as bees. They may be small, but they can **sting** very sharply. Most animals have four **limbs** plus a **tail**. But some, such as insects, may have six **limbs**. As for natural **phenomena**, there are many volcanoes. They can erupt with **overwhelming** force. Some volcanoes spread **ash** all throughout the air. That can cause problems on the entire planet. The Earth is truly amazing.

1. There are just a few galaxies in the universe. ________
2. There are many natural phenomena on the Earth. ________
3. Lions can sting people with their tails. ________
4. Volcanoes can spread ash into the air. ________

Unit 28 Word List

1 **cottage** [kátidʒ]

n. a small house, often by a lake or at a mountain (syn) lodge

rent a cottage

→ We rented a **cottage** by the lake last summer.

2 **dwell** [dwel]

v. to live in a certain place

dwell in

→ They have **dwelled** in the city for ten years.

3 **entire** [intáiər]
adv. entirely

adj. containing everything (syn) whole (ant) partial

entire life

→ She has lived in Korea for her **entire** life.

4 **fairly** [fέərli]

adv. justly, clearly, or honestly; to a slight degree

fairly done → The judging in the contest was **fairly** done.

fairly small → That dog is **fairly** small.

5 **fate** [feit]

n. something that happens and cannot be avoided (syn) destiny

believe in fate

→ Many people believe in **fate**.

6 **forefather** [fɔ́:rfɑ̀:ðər]

n. a person in one's family who lived in the past (syn) ancestor

one's forefather

→ Her **forefathers** lived in Italy many years ago.

7 **gradual** [grǽdʒəwəl]
adv. gradually

adj. taking place slowly or little by little

gradual development

→ The **gradual** development of the city lasted for ten years.

8 **holy** [hóuli]

adj. sacred, or related to God

holy book

→ The Bible is a **holy** book for Christians.

9 **impulse** [ímpʌls]

n. a sudden feeling that causes a person to act (syn) urge

feel an impulse

→ Ted felt a sudden **impulse** to stand up.

10 **occasion** [əkéiʒən]
adj. occasional

n. a certain, special, or important time

special occasion

→ His family sometimes eats out on special **occasions**.

11 **overall** [óuvərɔl]

adj. including or covering everything (syn) total

overall grade

→ His **overall** grade in the class was an A.

12 **predict** [pridíkt]

n. prediction

v. to make a guess about a future event (syn) forecast

predict the weather

→ It can be difficult to **predict** the weather.

13 **polish** [páliʃ]

v. to rub something to make it smooth and shiny

polish one's shoes

→ Mr. Jones **polishes** his shoes every day.

14 **procedure** [prəsíːdʒər]

n. a particular course or way of doing something

follow a procedure

→ Please follow the **procedure** to do it properly.

15 **rarely** [rέərli]

adv. not very often (syn) hardly

rarely rain

→ It **rarely** rains in the desert.

16 **react** [riǽkt]

n. reaction

v. to act in response to something

react to

→ How will you **react** to his comments about you?

17 **response** [rispάns]

n. an answer (syn) reply

give a response

→ She gave a **response** to Steve's email.

18 **remind** [rimáind]

v. to make a person remember

remind someone

→ Please **remind** me to finish my homework.

19 **strip** [strip]

strip - stripped - stripped

v. to take off clothing, a covering, etc.

n. a long, narrow piece of metal, wood, paper, etc.

strip off → He **stripped** off his clothes to take a shower.

metal strip → Doug fixed the problem by using a metal **strip**.

20 **swallow** [swάlou]

v. to take food or drink into one's body through the mouth

swallow food

→ **Swallow** your food after you chew it.

Unit 28 Exercise

A Match the words with their definitions.

1. cottage	a. to act in response to something
2. strip	b. a small house, often by a lake or at a mountain
3. procedure	c. to rub something to make it smooth and shiny
4. occasion	d. a particular course or way of doing something
5. react	e. sacred, or related to God
6. polish	f. a certain, special, or important time
7. holy	g. to take off clothing, a covering, etc.
8. impulse	h. a sudden feeling that causes a person to act

B Circle the two words in each group that have the same meaning.

1. a. ancestor	b. forefather	c. entire	d. occasion
2. a. react	b. destiny	c. remind	d. fate
3. a. hardly	b. cottage	c. dwell	d. rarely
4. a. impulse	b. total	c. overall	d. procedure

C Circle the words that best fit the sentences.

1. I predict | react the idea will be very popular.

2. She asked a question but got no impulse | response .

3. Please react | remind me to wake up early tomorrow.

4. They plan to dwell | polish in the countryside someday.

5. Martin ate the entire | gradual sandwich in two minutes.

6. His throat was so dry he could not swallow | dwell anything.

D Choose the correct words to complete the sentences.

1. The weather has been ______________ hot these days.
   a. gradual b. entire c. fairly d. occasion

2. The ______________ construction of the building was fun to watch.
   a. rarely b. gradual c. holy d. fate

3. His ______________ came from Norway and Sweden.
   a. impulses b. forefathers c. procedures d. fates

4. Jane's ______________ performance was the best of everyone.
   a. overall b. gradual c. fairly d. holy

5. She remembered to ______________ all of the silver plates.
   a. swallow b. react c. polish d. strip

E Read the passage. Then, fill in the blanks.

Hundreds of years ago, Mark's **forefathers** lived in Europe. They **dwelled** in Germany. However, they gave up their **entire** lives there and moved to another place. This place was America. In America, Mark's **forefathers** built a small **cottage** in a forest. Then, they created a large farm around the **cottage**. It was **fairly** difficult to make, but it was a beautiful place.

Today, Mark still lives in that **cottage**. He **rarely** goes into town because he loves living on his farm. On **occasion**, he thinks about his **forefathers**. He believes it was **fate** that they moved there. When people ask him if he will ever move, he gives the same **response**. He says, "This is **holy** land to me. I will live here for my **entire** life."

1. Mark's ______________ used to live in Germany.
2. Mark lives in a ______________ in a forest.
3. Mark thinks it was ______________ that his relatives came to America.
4. Mark plans to live on his farm for his ______________ life.

Unit 29 Word List

1 **beneath** [biníːθ]
prep. below or in a lower place (syn) under (ant) above
beneath something
→ The pen is **beneath** the notebook on the desk.

2 **constraint** [kənstréint]
n. something that limits another thing
advise constraint
→ Mr. Anderson advised **constraint** in this matter.

3 **convert** [kɑnvə́ːrt]
n. conversion
v. to change from one form to another
convert ~ to
→ Can you **convert** kilograms to pounds?

4 **deserve** [dizə́ːrv]
v. to earn or be worthy of through one's actions
deserve a prize
→ You **deserve** a prize for your hard work.

5 **enormous** [inɔ́ːrməs]
adj. very large (syn) huge (ant) tiny
enormous problem
→ The lack of jobs is an **enormous** problem now.

6 **formal** [fɔ́ːrməl]
adv. formally
adj. following the usual requirements or customs (ant) casual
formal clothes
→ **Formal** clothes include suits and dresses.

7 **graduate** *v.* [grǽdʒueɪt] *n.* [grǽdʒuət]
v. to complete a course of study at a school
n. a person who has finished studying at a school
graduate from → Marcia hopes to **graduate** from high school next year.
university graduate → Jim hopes to become a university **graduate**.

8 **heap** [hiːp]
n. a group of things on top of one another
heap of
→ There is a **heap** of books lying on the floor.

9 **hut** [hʌt]
n. a small house made of natural materials (syn) cabin
build a hut
→ Craig built a **hut** near the beach.

10 **neutral** [njúːtrəl]
adj. not with either side in a dispute, fight, etc.
neutral country
→ Switzerland has been a **neutral** country for many years.

11 **omit** [oumít]

v. to leave out or not mention (ant) include
omit a name
→ They **omitted** Tim's name from the guest list.

12 **previous** [príːviəs]
adv. previously

adj. happening or coming before something else (syn) prior
previous game
→ Our team won the **previous** game.

13 **primary** [práimeri]

adj. first or highest in rank or importance
primary color
→ Red, yellow, and blue are **primary** colors.

14 **refer** [rifə́ːr]
n. reference

v. to direct a person for information or something needed
refer to
→ You can **refer** to the dictionary for more information.

15 **sector** [séktər]

n. a part of a larger area, field, region, etc. (syn) zone
every sector
→ Every **sector** of the economy is doing well.

16 **secure** [sikjúər]
n. security

adj. free from danger or harm (syn) safe
secure computer
→ This is a **secure** computer that nobody can hack.

17 **sensible** [sénsəbl]

adj. having or using good judgment
sensible person
→ Carla is a very **sensible** person.

18 **solid** [sálid]

adj. hard; not in the form of a liquid or gas
become solid
→ Water becomes **solid** when it gets cold.

19 **somewhat** [sʌ́mhwʌ̀t]

adv. to some degree (syn) slightly
somewhat busy
→ Ms. Watson is **somewhat** busy this week.

20 **vow** [vau]

n. a promise
v. to make a promise (syn) swear
make a vow → He made a **vow** to his wife to be a good man.
vow to → Jim **vowed** to do his best on the test.

Unit 29 Exercise

A Circle the words that fit the definitions.

1. to earn or be worthy of through one's actions
   a. convert b. omit c. deserve d. vow
2. something that limits another thing
   a. constraint b. heap c. sector d. hut
3. to direct a person for information or something needed
   a. graduate b. refer c. vow d. convert
4. free from danger or harm
   a. secure b. enormous c. sensible d. primary
5. not with either side in a dispute, fight, etc.
   a. previous b. solid c. neutral d. formal

B Write S for synonym or A for antonym next to each pair of words.

1. ________ cabin – hut
2. ________ formal – casual
3. ________ previous – prior
4. ________ above – beneath
5. ________ slightly – somewhat
6. ________ include – omit

C Circle the words that best fit the sentences.

1. The wood is previous | solid and very strong.
2. She threw the trash on the floor in a big heap | hut .
3. He took a vow | sector to do his best all of the time.
4. The sensible | primary goal is to make a lot of money.
5. A calculator can convert | graduate from meters to feet.
6. Dinosaurs were formal | enormous animals that lived long ago.

D Choose the correct words to complete the sentences.

1. It will take Carla four years to ______________ from school.
   a. vow b. deserve c. graduate d. convert

2. The ______________ thing to do is to be patient.
   a. enormous b. sensible c. somewhat d. previous

3. We are entering an unexplored ______________ of the rainforest.
   a. constraint b. sector c. heap d. vow

4. The man lives in a small ______________ in the mountains.
   a. heap b. neutral c. refer d. hut

5. Do not ______________ any information when telling the story.
   a. omit b. vow c. deserve d. convert

E Read the passage. Then, write T for true or F for false.

In their youths, most people have **somewhat** similar lives. They study at school for a total of twelve years. Then, they **graduate** from high school. Some people are satisfied with their **previous** schooling. Others believe it is **sensible** for them to attend college. They decide to get four more years of **formal** education.

Once these people are college **graduates**, they start to look for jobs. They want secure jobs, so they **vow** to work only at the best companies. They believe they **deserve** to work at good places. They also want to work in **sectors** they are interested in. Sometimes their friends may **refer** them for good jobs. It takes an **enormous** amount of effort to do this. But most people think the effort is worth it.

1. Few people attend school for twelve years. ______
2. Some people think it is sensible to go to college. ______
3. People who want secure jobs vow to work at good companies. ______
4. Some people's family members refer them for good jobs. ______

Unit 30 Word List

1 **drift** [drift]

v. to move around slowly in the water or air

drift away

→ The log in the water **drifted** away down the river.

2 **eventual** [ivéntʃuəl]

adv. eventually

adj. happening sometime in the future

eventual success

→ You must work hard to get **eventual** success.

3 **further** [fə́:rðər]

adj. more; additional

adv. at or to a greater distance or degree (syn) farther

further help → John provided **further** help for his friends.

go further → She will go **further** than anyone else.

4 **incidence** [ínsidəns]

n. the rate of occurrence of something

high incidence

→ There was a high **incidence** of the flu last year.

5 **initial** [iníʃəl]

adj. relating to the beginning (syn) first

initial job

→ Mary's **initial** job was at a library.

6 **input** [ínpùt]

n. something that is put in

v. to enter information on a computer

helpful input → Tim provided helpful **input** on the project.

input data → It takes time to **input** data on the computer.

7 **operate** [ápərèit]

n. operation

v. to work like a machine does

operate a computer

→ Most people know how to **operate** a computer.

8 **oppose** [əpóuz]

n. opposition

v. to be or act against (ant) support

oppose someone

→ John **opposed** Shannon in the student election.

9 **partial** [pá:rʃəl]

adj. being only in part (ant) total

partial payment

→ Molly made a **partial** payment on her credit card.

10 **perhaps** [pərhǽps]

adv. possibly (syn) maybe

perhaps not

→ Maybe Jeff will come or **perhaps** not.

11 **permission** [pərmíʃən]

n. the act of being allowed to do something

permission slip

→ A parent must sign the **permission** slip to go to the zoo.

12 **portray** [pɔːrtréi]

v. to show in words, a painting, a drawing, etc.

portray as

→ He was **portrayed** as a kind person.

13 **reap** [riːp]

v. to take in crops from a field (syn) harvest

reap crops

→ The farmer will **reap** his crops this week.

14 **sip** [sip]

sip - sipped - sipped

v. to take a small drink of something

sip tea

→ Joy is **sipping** some tea in a café.

15 **sort** [sɔːrt]

n. a specific kind, type, species, etc.

v. to arrange according to a group or type

certain sort → I am looking for a certain **sort** of bicycle.

sort clothes → Please **sort** the clothes by color.

16 **spin** [spin]

spin - spun - spun

v. to move around in a circle

spin around

→ The gymnast can **spin** around many times.

17 **tame** [teim]

adj. no longer wild, like an animal (ant) wild

tame a lion

→ The circus uses **tame** lions in its shows.

18 **though** [ðou]

conj. in spite of the fact that (syn) although

even though

→ Even **though** Eric is happy, he is quitting his job.

19 **tremendous** [triméndəs]

adj. very great in size, amount, etc.

tremendous success

→ The movie was a **tremendous** success.

20 **twist** [twist]

v. to wind a rope, string, etc. around something else

twist a rope

→ Try not to **twist** the rope too much.

Unit 30 Exercise

A Match the words with their definitions.

1. eventual	a. happening sometime in the future
2. sort	b. something that is put in
3. tremendous	c. the act of being allowed to do something
4. input	d. a specific kind, type, species, etc.
5. portray	e. being only in part
6. partial	f. the rate of occurrence of something
7. permission	g. very great in size, amount, etc.
8. incidence	h. to show in words, a painting, a drawing, etc.

B Circle the two words in each group that have the same meaning.

1. a. perhaps	b. eventual	c. maybe	d. twist
2. a. reap	b. harvest	c. tame	d. portray
3. a. operate	b. partial	c. initial	d. first
4. a. further	b. spin	c. incidence	d. farther

C Circle the words that best fit the sentences.

1. Input | Sip your coffee because it is still hot.
2. Most dogs and cats are tame | initial animals.
3. He can operate | spin in a circle several times.
4. The logs are just drifting | opposing in the ocean.
5. We spin | oppose the new law that was just passed.
6. She is happy though | further she is busy at her job.

D Choose the correct words to complete the sentences.

1. I requested ______________ assistance on the project.

a. tame b. though c. further d. input

2. Do you know how to ______________ this machine?

a. spin b. operate c. portray d. sip

3. David ______________ the string and caused a big problem.

a. twisted b. sorted c. input d. opposed

4. He ______________ a lot of wheat from the field yesterday.

a. drifted b. spun c. operated d. reaped

5. ______________ that is not the best idea.

a. Further b. Though c. Initial d. Perhaps

E Read the passage. Then, fill in the blanks.

Mary has a **tremendous** problem. She wants a pet, but her father **opposes** the idea. She tells her father the animal will be **tame**. But he does not believe her. She goes to her mother for some **input**. Her mother asks Mary what **sort** of animal she wants. Mary does not know yet. Mary's mother tells her to do some research. Then, she can ask her father for **permission** again.

Mary borrows some books from the library and goes to a café. While **sipping** her drink, she reads the books. **Though** she learns a **tremendous** amount, she does not stop studying. Instead, she reads **further**. Finally, she talks to her father again. He no longer **opposes** her idea and gives her **permission**. He will let Mary have a pet cat.

1. Mary's father ______________ the idea of her having a pet.

2. Mary's mother provides some ______________ for Mary.

3. Mary ______________ a drink while reading some books.

4. Mary's father finally gives her ______________ to get a cat.

Review 06 Units 26~30

A Choose and write the correct words for the definitions.

portray	sector	counsel	solid
occasion	cottage	parallel	twist

1. a small house, often by a lake or at a mountain ➡ ______________
2. not in the form of a liquid or gas ➡ ______________
3. to give advice, opinion, or instruction ➡ ______________
4. a part of a larger area, field, region, etc. ➡ ______________
5. to wind a rope, string, etc. around something else ➡ ______________
6. a certain, special, or important time ➡ ______________
7. moving the same way but at the same distance and never meeting ➡ ______________
8. to show or depict in words, a painting, a drawing, etc. ➡ ______________

B Circle the words that are the most similar to the underlined words.

1. I would appreciate a <u>reply</u> by tomorrow morning.
   a. procedure b. cottage c. response d. fate

2. The two brothers have <u>separate</u> opinions on the matter.
   a. overwhelming b. shallow c. logical d. distinct

3. Whales are <u>huge</u> animals that live in the ocean.
   a. enormous b. previous c. primary d. sensible

4. The <u>manager</u> at the store works every day of the week.
   a. application b. boss c. vocation d. region

5. It is almost time to <u>harvest</u> the rice in the fields.
   a. sort b. drift c. input d. reap

C Choose the correct forms of the words to complete the sentences.

1. The entirely | entire movie was very entertaining.
2. They had an informal | informally talk during lunch.
3. We opposition | oppose the decision to cancel the parade.
4. The bank has a secure | security room that nobody can break into.
5. Some countries had colonize | colonies in Africa many years ago.

D Complete the sentences with the words in the box.

inputting
resign
predicted
shallow
omitted

1. The coach ______________ that his team would win the game.
2. She ______________ writing an answer to one question.
3. My father plans to ______________ in the next month.
4. He spent all night ______________ the data on the computer.
5. The children are swimming in the ______________ end of the pool.

E Write the correct phrases in the blanks.

retirement fund	university graduate	rarely rains
permission slip	hotel reservation	inherit money

1. The teacher gave every student a ______________________.
2. He will ______________________ when his parents pass away.
3. Melanie is the first ______________________ in her family.
4. It ______________________ in this country during the dry season.
5. Tom removed some money from his ______________________.
5. We canceled our ______________________ when we missed our flight.

F Circle the mistakes. Then, write the correct sentences.

1. This regional of the country gets very hot weather.

   ➡ ______________________________

2. Sue can be very slow to reaction sometimes.

   ➡ ______________________________

3. I trained hard to learn to operation the machine.

   ➡ ______________________________

4. The teacher asked the student to definition the word.

   ➡ ______________________________

5. It is easy to conversion grams to kilograms.

   ➡ ______________________________

G Complete the crossword puzzle.

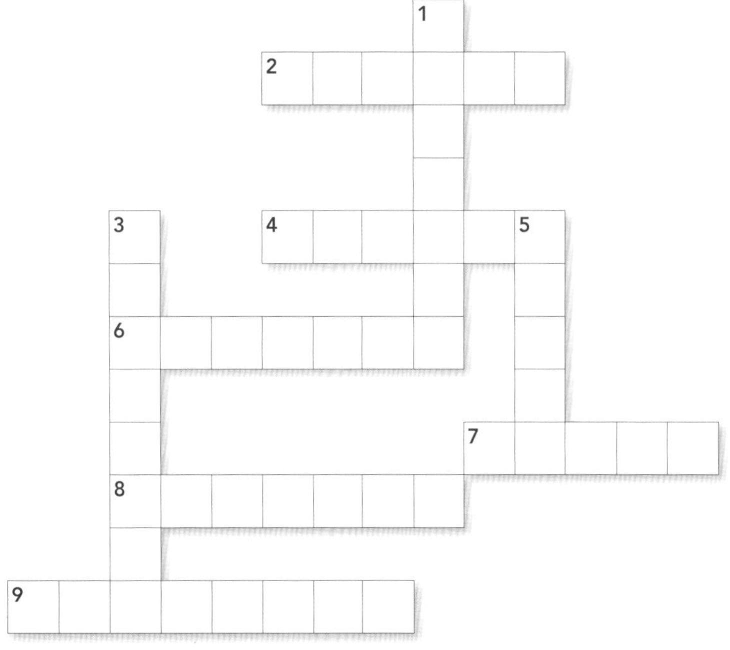

Across

2. a large group of stars
4. to make a person remember
6. in or near the middle
7. clear and easily understood
8. relating to the beginning
9. having or using good judgment

Down

1. being only in part
3. an occupation or business
5. to live in a certain place

H Read the passage. Then, answer the questions below.

Life in a Rural Region

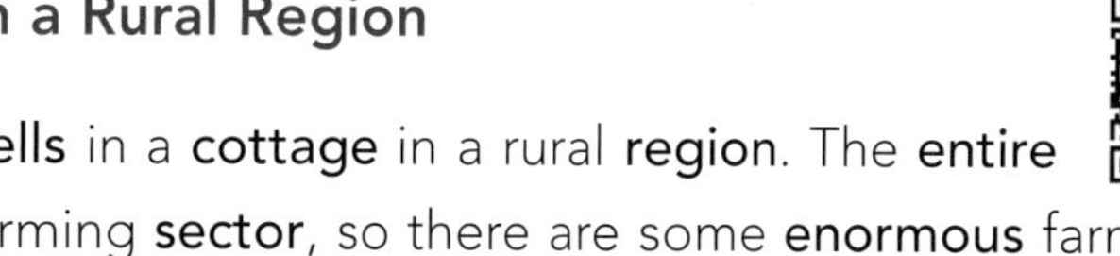

Lisa **dwells** in a **cottage** in a rural **region**. The **entire** area is a farming **sector**, so there are some **enormous** farms near her home. Lisa sometimes thinks about her **forefathers**. They lived in another country, but they **opposed** the government. They decided to leave, so they got **permission** to leave and went to Lisa's current home.

Lisa is a university **graduate** but does not want a **vocation** in a city. She never **submitted applications** to any companies. Instead, she **vowed** to return home. She enjoys the **distinct** lifestyle in the countryside. She can enjoy natural **phenomena** in a beautiful environment. She enjoys **sipping** tea and looking at her land a **tremendous** amount. Nature can be **overwhelming** at times, but Lisa has a **solid** and **secure** life.

1. What is the passage mainly about?

a. Lisa's vocation

b. Lisa's life

c. Life's university

d. Lisa's forefathers

2. Where is Lisa's cottage?

a. by a lake

b. in a big city

c. in another country

d. in a farming sector

3. What did Lisa vow to do?

a. return home

b. get a good job

c. build a cottage

d. apply to a company

4. Why did Lisa's forefathers leave their country?

➡ ______________________________

5. What does Lisa enjoy doing?

➡ ______________________________

Index

Index

A

B

C

D

E

Index

J

K

L

M

N

O

P

Index

Memo